Wicca

Witchcraft Moon Spells and
Wicca Book of Spells

2 Books In 1:

Everything You Want to Know About the
Lunar Phases and Magic Rituals. Practice
Witchcraft and Learn how to Create
Enchantments.

Linda Candles

Wicca

Text Copyright © Linda Candles

Legal & Disclaimer

TABLE OF CONTENTS
WITCHCRAFT MOON SPELLS

TABLE OF CONTENTS
WITCHCRAFT MOON SPELLS

Wicca

Witchcraft Moon Spells

How to use the Lunar Phase for Spells, Wiccan and Crystal Magic, and Rituals. A starter kit for Witchcraft Practitioners using the Mysteries of Herbs and Crystals Magic.

Linda Candles

Book Description

The moon has been a source of inspiration to human kind, and it has always had a very impactful position in the lore of the world throughout a number of different cultures across the world and throughout our history. The moon, as well as the sun, have both served very important purposes to us, and have seemingly always had very strong connections to the gods and goddesses that we have revered throughout human history. Similarly, to the sun, the moon is often associated with a large number of gods throughout the world from a number of different cultures. It is most commonly associated with a lot of the concepts and ideas that humans are commonly concerned with or about. Some of the most common and most significant of these associations are the spirit, soul, heart, fertility, passion, and love as well as death, the afterlife, and rebirth and a large number of different mysteries to humanity. Of course, the moon is still a very significant part of regular life even today, and is still present in modern belief systems like Wicca and other forms of paganism and modern witchcraft. Many wiccans will typically gather during the full moon in order to perform certain rituals that honor the wiccan goddess during each of the different Sebat's. Of course, the sun and the moon are not the only bodies that possess their own energy. The earth also acts as an independent source of energy, as well as receiving energy from the sun and the moon. However, it does still receive some energy from the moon and the sun, which allow for the creation and the ability to sustain the life on the earth. The energy that is produced by the moon is often thought to be "magnetic", in a sense, due to its size and proximity to the earth causing its gravitational pull to have a very strong impact on the life that exists on the earth. This is often the origin of the "pull" that some people will feel toward the moon on a clear night. Some people, if they are particularly sensitive to these kinds of forces, might even feel a literal tugging sensation within their bodies during the new or full moon, but most people will simply notice a slightly stronger kind of connection with the moon during these moments.

This book gives a comprehensive guide on the following:

- What is Wicca?
- World of Wicca
- The Energy of the Moon
- The Eight Phases of the Moon
- Moon magic of the lunar cycle
- What Do Wiccans Believes
- Life-Changing Moon Manifesting Visualization Strategy
- Simple Spells and Rituals... AND MORE!!!

Introduction

In the broadest sense, Wicca, also known as The Craft, is a term used to encompass most forms of modern Pagan Witchcraft. Many people don't know what it means to be Wiccan, or who a witch might be today. In the past, throughout history, witches have been persecuted for being agents of evil or even Devil worshippers. While Wiccans certainly aren't perfect, as are none of us, they are no more evil than any other group of people with the same spiritual views. For Wicca it is not the practice of satanic worship nor Devil worship, Wicca is, in essence, the exact opposite to this and has nothing to do with the Dark Arts, unlike these stereotyped folklores.

To many people's surprise Wiccans encompass a broad spectrum of people as well. A Wiccan could be a typical businessman, that performs rituals every week as a high priest in his coven, or that nice older lady who lives down the block, and always used to send you cookies when she heard you were feeling down (You had no idea she was giving you healing energies, too!). Wiccans are doctors, and handymen, housewives and rock stars. Wicca is a way of life that many people share and a community of giving and acceptance worldwide. Wiccans are those who share and practice these beliefs and ideals. Yet the religion has no recognition of hierarchy, leadership or sectarianism. The beauty of Wicca as a belief system is that it is not limited to one religion or one ideal, yet open to all systems of beliefs as an adaptation to your way of living, to enhance your current belief system. In a narrower definition, Wicca is a religion developed and descended from British Traditional Wicca (BTW), or Witchcraft. Its core practices and rituals have come together over time throughout history. Yet it was not until the early 19th Century that this world was bought to the public attention after centuries of being stigmatized.

Many people refer to Gerald Gardener, also known as Scare, to be the father of Wicca. Due to his original development and culmination of these ancient practices throughout the 1940s and 1950s that Gardner and later with collaboration by Doreen Valiente, into what is known today as Wicca. These two spiritual pioneers outlined and developed what would later come to be known as part of today's British Traditional Wicca, drawing on a wide, and sometimes highly disputed set of ancient Pagan and Hermetic belief systems. This included but never limited to tapping into Freemasonry, Druidism, Shamanic work, modern science and medicine, calling upon works of the likes of Aleister Crowley. Other spiritual leaders in the Wiccan and Pagan community would leave their indelible marks on the rich, varied and sometimes misunderstood spiritual faith called Wicca. From fierce opposition in the form of scathing British scorn to the New Age boom of Neo-Pagan and Wiccan theologies of the 1960s counterculture in the U.S.A. Two recent poles into American Religious Identification identify Wicca as one the fastest growing, evolving and ever-changing spiritual choice for millions of people.

The term Wicca itself is often disputed, yet has the roots to Anglo-Saxon language, meaning "wise one" this later was adopted in the Old English language to form term "witch," the term that many people have known practitioners of Wicca by for the last centuries. This original term was readopted due to the exploration into the ways of old and as a memoir back to the roots of Wicca's as a polytheistic belief system, as the word which was chosen by the Old British English and given a reputation for the Dark Arts throughout the Early Christian Era. Today, those who call themselves Wiccan are practitioners of a widely varied and diverse tradition, based in British Traditional Wicca, but encompassing many different offshoots and beliefs.

Chapter 1 What is Wicca?

Wicca is an active 20th century cult in contemporary witchcraft that helps its practitioners develop a deeper connection with Nature and Mother Earth. Through its teachings, the religion of Wicca promotes awareness, love and respect for the Sun and the sunlight, Moon, rivers, winds, rain and mountains, the animal kingdom, flowers and trees, the soil beneath our feet, the colorful autumn and the winter snow.

Wicca teaches us that everything that surrounds us is made of energy, and it embraces the principle of duality in all creation. This entails the existence of a God and Goddess, the masculine and feminine energy, the positive and negative. The whole Universe is made of such energy and Nature itself is a beautiful manifestation of the duality principle as we, human beings, hold the spark of duality within us.

In Wicca, Gods and Goddesses are within us and with us. Portrayed as much more mild and nurturing entities, they are not vengeful towards their children, they do not hold grudges and punish and do not create Heaven and Hell. Instead, they are ever loving, understanding and promote love and equality.

Wicca teaches us to accept full responsibility for our actions and does not support behavior and claims of an external entity such a Devil manipulating us into doing something bad.

This is where the teaching of Karma comes in and the idea that what you put out in the world comes back to you in the form of energy, people, and circumstances. Wiccans do not believe in

Satan or any other representation of Evil. Such concepts are usually part of Christian teachings. Also, there is no claim of any exclusivity in terms of it being the only path to knowledge, peace, wisdom and divinity. Instead, the teachings of Wicca encourage the individual to seek out and choose his or her own path in life. This philosophy is based on the belief that Nature is sacred and that Life deserves respect regardless of the form through which it is manifested.

Wiccan Spells

Wiccan spells are frequently portrayed into two noteworthy sorts, "White magic" being related with high and considerate points and "Dark Magic" regularly connected with abhorrence deeds and evil love.

Numerous advanced Wiccans have stopped utilizing this duality, contending that the shading dark is simply one more shading that has been performed by Hollywood, and that the shading itself ought not to have any relationship with sinister ceremony or hatred by any stretch of the imagination.

Wiccans accept that magic spell casting is a fundamental law of nature. A law that we still can't seem to get it. Different devotees of the Wicca Religion don't profess to know how their magic works by any stretch of the imagination, and it is sufficient that it does work and that they have seen it work for themselves.

Most Wiccans characterize Wiccan spells or Wiccan Magic as "the Art of making changes happen in consistence with one's very own will." The term Wiccan essentially alludes to any individual who practices the Wiccan Religion.

A Wiccan spell is training or ritualized occasion which prompts quantifiable changes in the physical or enthusiastic circle as per the aims of at least one Wiccans who are casting the spell.

Wiccan magic spells ordinarily rehearsed incorporate love spells, mending spells, ripeness spells just as spells to help evacuate any terrible impacts.

The Wiccan Sacred Circle

Wiccans regularly cast spells during ceremonial practices within a develop called "the Sacred Circle," trying to realize changes to their reality.

A Sacred Circle is a circle or circle of room stamped blessed by Wiccans to either contain vitality and structure a sacred space or to shape a hindrance of security. The Sacred Circle can sometimes be both.

Sacred Circles are made by making a ring from salt or chalk. A few Wiccans will even scratch a line in the earth, and now and again it can essentially be envisioned by a Wiccan Witch to deliver similar outcomes. Comparative round develops show up in some Eastern religions.

Wiccan spells, in most of the occasions, are cast to help emerge an altruistic outcome. The fact of the matter is most of the magic spells cast by Wiccans (just as numerous different adherents and supporters of the "Old Religions") are cast for good and not malicious.

The Law of Threefold Return

This is exhibited by the Wiccan Rede, which essentially expresses "it hurt none, do what ye will." Many Wiccans likewise have faith in another component of Wiccan ethical quality which is "The Law of Threefold Return."

This law holds that paying little mind to what sort of Wiccan spell is cast, be it big-hearted or pernicious, the activities of the spell will return to the practitioner with triple the power or power.

This belief is fundamentally the same as the eastern way of thinking of Karma, first embraced in quite a while and later showing up in different structures in the Buddhist, Jain, Sikh and Hindu methods of reasoning. This is one motivation behind why Wicca is consistently alluded to as the yoga of the west.

Yoga as a whole is one of the six schools of Hindu way of thinking. Yoga is about control and preparing working together to enable the awareness to arrive at a condition of impeccable profound knowledge and serenity. Numerous advanced Wiccans will see this announcement as a reasonable meaning of their belief systems too.

Wiccan Spells come in numerous sorts and varieties since you practice your spell casting with a decent and kind mental demeanor, you will discover like huge numbers of that the old nature religions, for example, Wicca can be fulfilling and as satisfying the same number of progressively eastern and western belief systems.

Instructions to Create Your Wiccan Spells

Digging Into Witchcraft

If you discover spells that you have turned out to be fairly enamored with, however, you would feel significantly more grounded about them if you could "change" a couple of things, you can utilize spells offered in books or on the web. As you adjust spells to suit your inclinations, there are a few things you'll have to consider. Above all else, recollect that if you are adapting spells from different works, your adjustments are for your utilization as it were. A ton of agnostic journalists offer spells for adjustment; however, you certainly would prefer not to encroach on the copyright of writers or online scholars by sharing your adjusted works on the web or off, particularly without the consent from the first writers of the adjusted work.

Before you start composing or adapting spells by any means, ensure you consider what it is that you truly need; "watch what you wish for" is inferred here. Ensure you are clear about what you need, yet why you need it, and how you anticipate that your wants should manifest. You ought to likewise give full thought to any potential outcomes of your magickal workings; sometimes when you are working magick, you can wind up with the result that gives you decisively what you requested, yet not how you anticipated. This is why specificity is so essential to work.

Regardless of whether you are adapting spells you have turned out to be partial to or composing your spells without any preparation, you'll have to keep your aim in the back of your psyche. Each word in the spell needs to line up with your goal and the desired outcome. To that end, how specific you are with your spells will characterize the achievement of your spell casting tries. To loan to the specificity in your compositions, you can consummate the wording and timing of the work, and you can utilize magickal correspondences.

Timing - Some practitioners time a spell is working during a specific moon stage. For example, you can time spells during the waxing, full, or melting away moon stage. The waxing moon is related with beginnings and the winding down the moon with endings, while the full moon is related with all magickal workings. Along these lines, if you are directing a spell where you need a circumstance to end, you can time your work for when the winding down moon shows up, and if you are searching for another beginning in a circumstance, the waxing moon is the best time to play out your work. A few practitioners likewise time their work dependent on days of the week, the season, the planetary hours, or mysterious correspondences.

Rhymes - Not all spells rhyme, yet you may find that you are undeniably progressively open to working with rhyme. You'll see it simpler to recall, and when utilizing rhyme, you make a mood with your words when expressed so anyone might hear. When you compose your very own spells, you ought to invest some energy retaining what you've composed. Along these lines, you can give your complete consideration to what words you are expressing as opposed to understanding them from a bit of paper.

Perception - Your spell ought to contain exact wording that won't just help you verbally express your wants, yet you'll additionally need wording that triggers your representation capacities. The more seriously you can picture your desired manifestation, the more noteworthy the probability you will accomplish the outcome you look for. Indeed, before working a spell, it's a smart thought investing some energy picturing your desired outcome. Similarly, as with your spell's wording, when imagining, you should be as specific as could be allowed, seeing your desired outcome in each conceivable detail.

Inspiration - Finally, if you're a Witch rehearsing the Wiccan religion, you'll need to ensure that your spell's wording and expected outcome is lined up with the Wiccan Rede of, "hurt none, do what ye will." As a Wiccan practitioner, you ought to be worried about the Threefold Law of Return and the potential kickback that goes with the demonstration of conveying negative energies. Ensure your spell workings are sure with the goal that what returns to you in the method for manifestation is similarly positive.

How to become a wiccan

1. Peruse

Before you even consider changing over to Wicca, or before you settle on any concluded choices or statements, you ought to invest some energy contemplating. Sorry to learn this— however if you don't care for perusing or considering, you're most likely not going to like Wicca without question; or possibly you're not going to get much of anywhere. Wicca is a non-dogmatic religion; as opposed to disclosing to you what to accept, it tosses the ball in your court and guides you to think fundamentally. This requires information.

One book isn't sufficient, yet five or ten books is a decent start. It's by and large prescribed you read and study—effectively— for in any event a year and a day before settling on any choices about whether to be Wiccan or not.

Step 2: Think

When you genuinely start finding out about Wicca, it's beliefs, it's precepts, and so forth., it's time to think about whether your beliefs are a match. Are your own beliefs something that can fall inside a Wiccan system?

Wicca is certainly not a dogmatic religion, and this is valid; so, anybody coming into it searching for a book of a sacred text or a rundown of charges is moving toward it from an inappropriate edge. In any case, Wicca is additionally not, as some more unfortunate sources have generally been putting it, "anything you need it to be." The issue with saying Wicca is anything is that you're saying it's nothing. There are a few things that don't fit very well under the definition.

For instance, if you don't have faith in any Gods, and you're simply hoping to practice enchantment, at that point why are you joining a religion in which the real rituals, celebrations, customs, and so on are focused on Pagan Gods and Goddesses? You could feel free to examine Witchcraft without getting to be Wiccan by any means. Or on the other hand, if you put stock in Jesus with your entire existence as a hero, why would you like to worship him inside a religion that instructs there is not something to be spared from?

The excellence of Wicca is that there are no commands—there are no 'acknowledge this or clear out' ways of thinking. In any case, in being a piece of an experiential religion, you are tolerating obligation to utilize rationale and reason—which means genuinely considering if your beliefs fit inside Wicca, or that if maybe a couple of things that draws in you to Wicca can be found in another religion that is more in accordance with your beliefs.

Step 3: Pray

When you come to the heart of the matter at which you realize you need to adore as a Wiccan, it's time to begin reversing. Start going to your Gods. Acquaint yourself and ask them to uncover themselves to you — request direction, for clarification, for comprehension.

Start ruminating—for as is commonly said, if supplication is conversing with your God, reflection is tuning in. An everyday reflection system can be gainful for wellbeing and health purposes, yet spiritual advancement.

Step 4: Observe

Start monitoring life from a Wiccan viewpoint. Watch the cycles of the seasons and the cycles of the moon. Start recognizing them in little ways. Consider Wiccan precepts and morals when you're looked with decisions. Think about your life, and territories in which exercises can be gained from Wicca.

Watch your general surroundings; the transaction between every living thing. Begin to see the cycles of the seasons, of the moon, of life. You may wish to get into an increasingly ordinary everyday practice with your reflections and supplications or start some extremely straightforward, casual rituals to observe Esbats and Sabbats.

Now, perusing and learning shouldn't stop, yet it's critical to begin some utilization of those standards. That is how you start living Wicca.

Step 5: Build

A misstep many individuals make right off the bat is hurrying out to gather tools—however, Wicca isn't a scrounger chase. In any case, now, when you've started to practice, you might need to begin moving towards progressively formal practice. You may wish to begin gathering special raised area tools—you don't need to get them at the same time. It's a smart thought to examine a tool and its motivation, at that point, search for it, begin to utilize it, doing this each in turn.

Many books will guide you to get various things; however, remember that you won't need each tool that each book refers to. This is why it's critical to comprehend a tool's capacity before you even stress over getting it—it might end up being something you needn't bother with.

It's likewise time to start fabricating your ritual. That is, building an increasingly organized way to deal with your ritual. That doesn't mean you need to design every single detail out; however, by its very definition, a ritual is a rehashed demonstration. The redundancy encourages you to arrive at ritual cognizance. It helps you to sidestep the condition of awareness where you're effectively thinking into that state in which you go into 'autopilot' with the goal that you can open yourself to the different energies you're attempting to raise.

Start pondering a standard opening and shutting, summons, throwing a circle. Once more, it's not something you need to do across the board night. However, every couple of months consider and include another component.

Step 6: Magic

Enchantment isn't the focal point of Wicca. However, it's positively a noteworthy segment. In the end, you're going to need to join some into your practice. Somebody intrigued by simply learning enchantment doesn't need to be Wiccan and ought to go directly to learning The Craft; however, if Wicca as a religion is the thing that premiums you, invest the energy acclimating yourself with the religion first. When you come to the heart of the matter at which you're gathering tools and holding standard rituals, it's a decent time to begin rehearsing this intriguing and charming component. Begin including some minor mysterious functions in your hover, just as beginning examinations in expressions of the human experience.

Step 7: Network

Sooner or later, it's beneficial for you to get out in the Pagan people group on the loose. There is no need to hold up until the conclusion to do this, yet if you haven't, yet, you should attempt now.

Meet with different Wiccans, go to classes or open rituals or drumming circles. Doing this can open you to numerous new thoughts, help you discover individuals to converse with that you can identify with, you may even discover a coven that you'd like to join if this is your definitive objective. Religions are close to home adventures, but on the other hand, they're intended to be experienced publicly somewhat.

This rundown is in no way, forms or shapes the best way to approach getting to be Wiccan, and however, if you're uncertain of where to begin or where to go, it's a decent progression that will get you on your way.

Wiccan rituals

Regardless of whether the event is a Sabbat, an Esbat, or an achievement, for example, a handfasting (wedding), a commencement, or a part of the arrangement, covens and circle individuals will assemble to love together, respect the Goddess and God, and commend the marvels to be found in the progressing cycles of life. While most Wiccan rituals are apprehended in private, a few covens will every so often hold theirs out in the open, with the goal that all who wish to watch can come and get familiar with the Craft. Many Wiccan circles do likewise, and may even welcome people in general to take part.

Solo rituals are no less significant, and single Wiccans realize that as they worship at each point along the Wheel of the Year, they include their light and power to the group supernatural energy on these exceptional events.

RUDIMENTS OF WICCAN RITUALS

Beautiful, baffling, rich, and encouraging, Wiccan rituals can take a wide range of structures, with no two occasions being similar. Some might be exceptionally organized and expound. This is frequently the situation with coven rituals, and however since most covens keep the subtleties of their rituals mystery, known uniquely to started individuals, it's difficult to depict them with much precision. Different rituals, especially those practiced by solitary and diverse Wiccans, might be genuinely basic by correlation, and may even be made up on the spot.

The substance of some random Wiccan ritual will rely upon the event. For instance, Esbats, or Full Moon festivities, are focused exclusively on the Goddess, while Sabbats respect the co-inventive connection between the Goddess and the God. In spite of all the potential varieties, be that as it may, there are a couple of essential elements that will, in general, be incorporated into what we may call a "common" ritual.

To begin with, there is a purification, both of the celebrant(s) and where the ritual is held. This can occur as a ritual shower, or potentially a smearing service to expel any unwanted energies from the ritual space, regardless of whether it's an outside territory or inside the home. Smearing includes the consuming of sacred herbs, for example, sage, rosemary, as well as lavender.

Setting up the altar comes straightaway. A few Wiccans can keep an altar forever set up in their homes, however even for this situation, and it will probably be enhanced differently relying upon the event, for example, acquiring fall foliage for Mabon (the Autumn Equinox) or Samhain (otherwise called

Halloween.) The altar is organized with the different Wiccan tools, images, and contributions, spread out as indicated by any of various traditions.

Next comes the throwing of the circle, a demonstration that makes a limit between the sacred space and the common, commonplace world. The altar is commonly at the focal point of the circle, with a lot of space for all required to work openly inside the circle, with no inadvertent venturing outside of the energetic limit. The circle might be set apart with sea salt, a long line, a few stones, herbs, or candles. There are numerous techniques for circle-throwing, which you can peruse progressively about here.

When the circle is thrown, the summons start. The order here can shift, however regularly the God and Goddess are welcome to join the ritual, and after that, the four Elements—Earth, Air, Fire, and Water—are summoned, as these are the crude materials that make up all of the presence. (In numerous traditions, a fifth Element—Akasha, or Spirit—is additionally brought in.) In different traditions, this progression is known as Calling the Quarters, and the four bearings (North, East, South, and West) are tended to, either rather than or notwithstanding the Elements.

When these means have occurred, the core of the ritual starts. To begin with, the aim of the event is expressed—regardless of whether it's to commend a Sabbat or an Esbat, or maybe to request of the God and Goddess for the benefit of somebody who needs mending or some other sort of help. (Enchanted spellwork can to sure be the focus of a ritual. However, numerous Wiccans will do this independently from Sabbat festivities, to maintain the focus on the Goddess and God during Sabbats.)

After the goal is expressed, the principle body of the ritual may comprise of different exercises. The point of convergence might be the presentation of a ritual show, for example, reenacting scenes from antiquated fantasies or ballads—or other ritualistic material, contingent upon the tradition of Wicca the gathering is following. Solitary Wiccans may likewise peruse from antiquated otherworldly messages, or make their very own verse for the event. Reciting, singing, moving and additionally other ritual motions might be a piece of the procedures, as might just thinking about casually the gifts of the season. Petitions may be offered, regardless of whether they are personal or for the benefit of others. It's basic in certain traditions to utilize ritual space to expect to help a whole network or even all of humanity.

In numerous traditions, a service known as "cakes and beer" (or "cakes and wine") is a significant piece of Wiccan rituals. Sustenance and drink are offered and emblematically imparted to the God and Goddess, ordinarily toward the part of the arrangement of the ritual (albeit a few traditions start with it). This function associates the spiritual plane with the Earth plane, and grounds and focus the members before shutting the ritual procedures. When it's an ideal opportunity to part of the arrangement, Elements and the Goddess and God are officially expressed gratitude toward and discharged, and the circle is shut.

Once more, this is only an essential format that a Wiccan ritual would commonly pursue. If you join a setup coven or circle, the gathering will in all probability have its very own rendition of what's been depicted above, with numerous potential varieties. If you're a solitary specialist, you can research a specific tradition to pursue, or you can make your very own interesting Wiccan rituals. For whatever length of time that your aim is earnest and you are focused on your activities, there's no real way to get it "wrong"!

Pretty much every religion joins sacred items into its recognition and practice. Regardless of whether its uncommon vestments worn by religious officiants, statues of gods respected at sanctuaries, candles, talismans, chalices or other emblematic items, individuals have been making and using physical artifacts—or "tools"— to make and keep up spiritual energy and focus in their ritual practices.

Wicca includes the utilization of a few tools, every one of which has its representative significance, specific uses, and specific situation on the Wiccan altar during a ritual.

A "HANDS-ON" PHILOSOPHY

Wiccan ritual tools are utilized to focus and direct spiritual (or "mystic") energy for the reasons for interfacing legitimately with the perfect. There's an unobtrusive yet significant qualification, nonetheless, between this practice and the utilization of emblematic items in different religions. Wiccans perceive that they share in the co-innovative powers of nature as typified by the Goddess and God, instead of being subject to the desire of a higher power.

This way, the tools of Wiccan ritual are both emblematic and down to earth, as each article and each activity performed inside the circle of sacred energy is intentionally expected to tackle and direct this co-imaginative power. Tools are utilized to summon and invite divinities and the energies of the Elements, to perform mystical work, and to secure against undesirable energetic impacts, among different capacities. Notwithstanding, it's critical to perceive that the tools don't have supernatural powers all by themselves—they function an source of the personal power of the Wiccan who uses them.

"THE LIST" OF WICCAN TOOLS

The precise arrangement of ritual tools viewed as at the center of Wiccan practice will change contingent upon the tradition. A few covens and solitaries watch exceptionally expand rituals utilizing an assorted cluster of articles, while others keep things generally basic, utilizing a few tools for various ritual capacities. That being stated, the most regularly referred to tools utilized in an essential ritual is the chalice (or cup), the wand, the pentacle, the athame (or ritual knife, articulated "a-that-may"), the censer (for incense), and at least one candles.

Other as often as possible referenced tools—which, once more, might be viewed as basic tools relying upon tradition—are the broom, the cauldron, the ringer, the sword, the staff, and the ritual scourge. Besides, there are various items that add to ritual however are not considered "tools" all by themselves, for example, pictures of the God and Goddess, a boline (an exceptional knife utilized for cutting and cutting), a plate for ritual nourishment and additionally different contributions, precious stones and herbs, altar materials and beautifications, and so on.

It's not in the slightest degree essential to have these things in your own to begin rehearsing Wicca. It's by and large prescribed to start little, get tools each or two in turn, and steadily construct your ritual practice as you go.

STARTING POINTS OF RITUAL PRACTICE

To individuals new to Wicca, these tools can appear to be, to some degree, irregular and discretionary. Why are things like blades, cups, ringers, and pentacles regarded fundamental for communing with soul energy? There are numerous potential responses to this inquiry, at the end of the day it requires some investment, study, and tolerance all together for the tools of ritual to make genuine "sense" to an expert. This is a major piece of the purpose behind the custom of reading for a year and a day before committing oneself to the practice of Wicca. What's more, it realizes as much as you can about the historical backdrop of Wicca's improvement, just as the numerous spiritual traditions it draws from, some of which go back to the relic.

Chapter 2 World of Wicca

What many people all around the world don't understand is that Wicca is an actual religion, also known as 'Benevolent Witchcraft', 'The Old Religion', and 'The Craft'. This ancient craft is a part of our modern paganism or is also known as nature spirituality.

Paganism is a name for those who follow a religion or practice which is not Christianity, Judaism, Buddhism, or Hinduism. The Wiccan religion is a part of Paganism along with Pantheists, Heathens, Goddess Spirituality folk, Ecofeminist, Unitarian Universalist Pagans, Animists, Druids, ChristoPagans, and any other Nature related spirituality practices.

But within those religions, there are a variety of groups, all with different purpose, practices, size, orientation, structure, and symbology. There are many different types of practices within the Wiccan religion, such as Shamanic, Alexandrian, British Traditionalist, Gardnerian, Faerie, Hereditary or Family tradition, Celtic, Circle Crat, Dianic, Eclectic Craft, and many other paths and traditions.

Certain of those groups have other different specific practices and groups. Some of the Wiccan religion groups are initiatory, while there are others who are not. Many of those initiatory practices vary from different traditions; several of those groups have initiations by spiritual helpers, teachers, groups, and deities within dreams, visions, and vigils quests.

There are many differences between a variety of groups and religions, but they all respect and love Nature. Many seek to live in peace and harmony with the world and the ecosystem around them. Many practitioners are able to communicate and become friends with many plants, animals, and spirits that occupy the Earth along with us. They even honor the natural cycles of nature, such as the new moon and the full moon. Many love to perform rituals during these times, harnessing the energy of the element of earth. Those who follow the Wiccan religion are referred to as 'witches'.

In this Wiccan religion and other Paganism religions, it's a belief that every human, stream, animal, rock, tree, and other forms of nature possess a Divine Spirit located within. This is why in many traditions, apart from Paganism, they have a monotheistic dimension in which there is only one Divine God that they worship. In Paganism and some other traditions, they have a polytheistic dimension in which there are a variety of Divine forms including Gods, Goddesses, and many other spiritual forces. Nature and the universe play a big role in the way the Wiccan religion is shaped.

Chapter 3 The Energy of the Moon

The energy of the moon and the sun have shaped our development throughout our history, as well. Humans, as well as all other forms of life on earth, all maintain a strong connection to the energies of our celestial bodies, especially with the moon, which is the origin of a lot of the sensations and feelings that we will often refer to as our "intuition", which is why many people will consider women to be more naturally intuitive than men; they have a much stronger connection to the feminine energies that the moon emits, resulting in their higher level of intuitive talent compared to men.

This sensitivity to the energies of the sun and the moon are often referred to as our "sixth sense", and is arguably one of the most significant tools that we have access to when practicing any form of magic but this applies specially to moon magic.

When we are practicing moon magic, one of the most common ways to begin is to "appeal" to the moon and form a connection to it for the duration of the spell, but this connection that is formed is somewhat false; what is really happening is that the connection that we already possess with the moon is strengthened as we open ourselves up to the moon's energy and allow the pathway formed by this energy to be increased in size.

When this is done in the presence of the moon, and especially during the periods of the full moon and the new moon, when its power is strongest, this connection will allow us to greatly strengthen the spells and other kinds of magical work that we perform.

It is important to understand, however, that the different phases of the moon will produce slightly different energies that will be useful for different kinds of purposes or for different kinds of spells.

Each of the different phases of the moon carries a different kind of energy, which can be useful for different kinds of magic, and to accomplish different kinds of goals.

Our relationship with the moon about the magic that we perform with the energy that it provides us with seems to wax and wane with the different phases of the moon itself.

As the moon is waxing, its energy moves toward its peak and it will be able to much more effectively serve magic that is meant to increase potential or energy, while the magic that is performed during the later half of the lunar cycle is best used for magic that is meant to decrease the strength of energies or potential, such as banishing or cleansing unwanted energies.

The middle point during the cycle of the moon is commonly referred to as the harvest, and is the time to celebrate for the accomplishments that have been made and the spoils that have been reaped from the first part of the lunar cycle, similarly to the harvest that it is named for.

The second half of the lunar cycle is then dedicated to cleaning up after the fact and releasing the energies and the things that are not needed any more.

During the new moon, new intentions are set for the new cycle which will be manifested in the same way and ultimately dismissed as we move on to the cycle after that.

The lunar cycle ultimately represents a progression through time following a healthy course of events that allow for the creation of new things that will eventually be removed in order to allow more new things to be made in an endless cycle of renewal.

There are also a few basic tips for how to further empower the magical work that you perform at different points throughout the different stages of the cycle of the moon. For example, the first stage of the lunar cycle is the new moon. During the new moon, the energy that we receive from the moon will be particularly well suited for setting intentions for the rest of the month or for thinking about the things that you might want to build. Starting new tasks or projects will be much more effective during this phase of the moon's cycle, and any magical work that you perform involving the attraction of specific energies will be very effective during this period.

The second phase, when the moon will be rising to its highest point when it is full, is referred to as the waxing moon. This is the best phase of the lunar cycle for utilizing the energies that we receive from the moon in order to help us in moving forward toward the goals that we have set. This is the next logical step after starting up new projects, to move forward and to take action in order to begin to accomplish those goals.

The energy that you receive during this phase will be especially helpful for allowing us to reach the goals that we may have set, and can be very effective if it is applied to spell work that is related to the increase of various different kinds of energies. Some common examples are strengthening or building bonds between or among different people, or improving the physical or mental health.

The stage opposite to the waxing moon is the waning moon. This phase comes immediately after the full moon and before the new moon. The energy that you will receive during the full moon will be best for purposes opposite to the energy of the waxing moon.

The spellwork that you perform with the energy of the waning moon will be best used for things like releasing energies in order to overcome obstacles in your path or for cleansing yourself of negative energies.

The phase of the lunar cycle that is often considered the one that contains the most powerful energy is the full moon. Many people will believe the full moon to be the most magically significant day of the lunar cycle, and will take the opportunity to use the energy of the full moon for spells that are especially important. This is the reason for legends of werewolves or vampires, or a number of other kinds of supernatural or magical beings and events occurring on the night of the full moon.

This is when the moon and its power are at their highest points, and will be much more universally effective than during the other phases of the moon's cycle.

The moon's cycles start with the new moon. At this time the moon and sun are perfectly aligned but the sun's reflection faces away from Earth and this is why we can't see her glowing.

During this time the moon will rise and set during the day and it is sometimes impossible to see her without using a telescope. New beginnings and the new moon are pretty much the same things.

During these times, you need to focus on the things you want to manifest in your life such as new intentions and projects.

Harnessing the New Moon's Energy. Being able to visualize is the main key here. Where your thoughts go, your energy will flow. You have to bring awareness to the energy you are working with and the things you want to bring to life. If you have conscious thoughts and can direct your intentions and energy, everything you want in life is possible.

Create a Vision Board. You have to make your desires tangible things. Things that you can touch, look at and bring to life.

This can be done with poster board, magazine clippings, and glue or you can go digital and make a board on Pinterest. Your goal is to put all your intentions in one place.

When you have finished the board, look at each item and imagine the steps you need to take to make it happen. Will this take a lot of work? Will you need to ask for help from others? What do you need to do to get things moving?

Find some inspiration by defining the process for every intention. Inspiration will build momentum and momentum brings results.

Make a Sigil and Burn It. Sigils are a great way to get creative while pouring your intentions, energy, and love into your work.

The first thing you do is find some pieces of paper and start writing out statements that you want to manifest during the moon's cycle.

After you have your statement, take it just as it is stated and think about all the outcomes that might be possible. It might say: "I would like to live in abundance."

That's fine and dandy but the abundance of what? Do you want an abundance of negativity? Would you like to have an abundance of weight? You have to get specific. If you were to say: "I want to live a healthy, happy life full of abundant love".

This is a lot clearer, isn't it? Once you send these out into the Universe there can't be any confusion about what you are setting fire to. Try to keep away from using alternate definition if at all possible. Now that you have your intention, it is time to write it again without any spaces and get rid of all the vowels and any letters that repeat. It would look something like:

"wntlvhypfbd"

This is a bit hard to read, isn't it? Now from this point, you begin to combine the words to make a symbol. Place the legs and arms in places they shouldn't be and let your creative juices flow. There aren't any wrong symbols. By the time you are through, it should feel right. If it doesn't, start over and work it until it does feel right.

Once you have it, it is something that has taken your love, intention, attention, and time. You have worked both sides of the brain to make this wish. Within the first three days of the moon's cycle, so you can harness the moon's energy, you need to burn it to release your power and intentions out into the Universe to start manifesting.

Momentum and the Waxing Moon. There are three phases of the waxing moon and all of them have to do with getting yourself ready to achieve and receive your new intentions.

Waxing Gibbous Moon: During this time, you need to redefine your goals and get in tune with them. Use what has happened during the past few weeks to figure out what you need to do to refine your intentions. Things should be a lot clearer because you have taken steps and gotten insight on your goals and how they are coming along.

First Quarter Moon: This is the best time to take action. Figure out the steps you need to do to reach your goals. Don't get off course when an obstacle arises. You have to push forward during this time.

Waxing Crescent Moon: During this time, you need to imagine and plan your intentions. Send your desires, dreams, and hopes out into the world and focus on ways these things are going to affect your life.

Harvest Time. Things have already been set in motion from this and other new moons. This is the best time and it is waiting for you to cash in all your gifts. Look at what is sitting right in front of your face.

Have any opportunities presented themselves to you that you might have missed? Do you feel a force pushing you in new directions?

You have to be vigilant, aware, and open. You have to listen with your heart to be able to hear what the moon has to say. She has the power, wisdom, and words to transform your life.

Harnessing the Full Moon's Energy. The moon's energy is most powerful when she is full. Visualization is great during a new moon.

Charging yourself physically is great during the full moon. Get outside and greet the beautiful full moon with an open soul, mind, and heart.

This is the time for positive opportunities if you know how to use it right. It could increase your positive energy, or it could create havoc with your emotions.

Because the full moon brings a lot of energy, you have to make sure your mind is calm in order to receive all the positive effects. Remember that whatever is happening to your spirit, mind, or body is going to be amplified tremendously.

If you feel angry, you are going to feel even angrier. If you feel happy, you are going to feel even happier.

When the moon is full, the ocean will swell, and the emergency rooms will always have more patients. Her energy is extremely powerful so make sure you direct it along with positive intentions.

Loving energy and crazy energy will all be intensified. Just know that this is a great opportunity for you to grow spiritually and emotionally.

Here are some ways for you to use the full moon's energy to bring good things into your life:

Send out blessings to people who need it. Because the full moon's power is behind you, you can send the pink light of loving to strangers, colleagues, family, and friends along with forgiveness, and healing energy. You can also send peaceful energy out into the world that might be experiencing war, poverty, hardship, and strife. It will give them a lot of benefits and you have just created a huge load of karma. During a full moon is the best time to do acts of kindness and be of service to others.

Meditate. When you pray, you are speaking with your god. When you meditate, you are allowing these gods to talk to you. Bathe in the moon's glow and just breathe. Meditate as long as your body can take it and drink in all the connections, energy, and wisdom that is flying through the universe toward you. Because the full moon gives off so much energy, you need to create stillness, mindfulness, and calm. This can be done alone or in a sacred space.

You can also connect with other friends or a group. You should be able to find a spiritual center, yoga studio or online group that will come together to meditate during a full moon. This is extremely powerful when you meditate in a group. The ocean's tides are highest during this time and this means your tide will be high, too. You need to use this to get those messages; otherwise, they will just be falling on closed ears.

Visualize your dreams being manifested. During the full moon is a great time to work on your manifesting techniques. Take some time to imagine your goals and they write them down on paper. It is also a good time to look at your vision board to see if you need to make any changes.

Make sure your vision board is where you can see if every day. Take the time to focus on your dreams during the full moon to give them an extra boost.

Be positive. Everyone knows we need to think positively as often as possible during a full moon so you will have the wind at your back. Positive thoughts get multiplied and energized. Even if you just take five minutes after you get up and right before you go to bed to think about all the positive things you have in your life, you will be doing a great thing for your life. You could write out a gratitude list.

You could write the Universe a thank you note for everything you have received. Look at yourself in the mirror and tell yourself nice things. Talk a walk and see all the beauty around you. Visualize your positive thoughts have been sprinkled with the glitter of the full moon to make them grow larger and larger.

Don't get angry or argue. You have to stay calm during the full moon. You have to forgive others, breathe deeply during difficult moments, and let things go. If you can't let things go, you have to communicate them with others. Try to postpone talking about what has upset you until the full moon has been gone for two days. The things that happen during this time gets multiplied. It is like pouring fertilizer on your emotions. Keep your energy moving in an uplifting, happy direction whether you are in your car, work, home, and in all your daily interactions.

Family and Friends Bonfire. Have someone play the drums, be present, breathe, and dance around the flame's energy. I was told by an elder that the spirits will see you better by the light of a fire, so make sure you are lighting the way for your spirit guides to find you so they can give you their message. Make sure you are willing and ready to receive it.

Release and the Waning Moon. Just like the waxing moon, there will be three waning moons' during the month. Everyone will help you move toward surrendering and releasing the Universe's plan along with your fate.

Waning Crescent: This is the last phase of the moon's cycle and it has the lowest vibrations. You might feel exhausted and drained, but this is completely normal during this phase. This phase wants you to recuperate and relax because you have cut ties with things that have been holding you back. While it is normal to feel tired, it is also important to surrender to any feelings you may have.

Feel them, heal them and move on. You are trying to manifest greatness and it will take some hard decisions and hard work.

Third Quarter: This is the best time for release. Are there things that are holding you back from reaching your ultimate goals?

Is it a relationship? A job? A project that has been sucking your life out of you? Find all the things that are taking away your creativity and energy. Start getting rid of these things. If something isn't serving your greater purpose, now's the time to get it out of your life.

Waxing Gibbous: Now is the time for inner reflection and introspection. Review your goals by turning inward. Make sure you have the right intentions to pursue everything that is in your line of vision. Are the things you do for the correct reasons? Will the goals you have set serve the greater good in your life? Reflect on what your goals are and redefine them if you need to.

There isn't any reason why you have to wait until the start or end of a moon cycle to begin using her energy. You can begin anytime and any day you would like. Find the moon phase for your area and jump in with both feet.

Look at how the moon has already affected your life and use her energy to move you forward in the flow of the Universe.

Wicca

Chapter 4 The Eight Phases of the Moon

I see the moon and the moon sees me." Women have always had a profound connection with the moon. Women crave their mystic properties, guidance, and attention. We yearn for it, just like other people yearn for daylight.

The moon makes us feel powerful. We gain strength and energy from her presence. We just need to learn how to live during each phase of the moon.

The moon is thought of as female in astrology. She presides over our monthly cycles, emotions, and fertility. All females can be affected by her pull. It recedes and renews just like the tides.

We feel drawn between times of introspection and introversion and we have moments of extreme energy and passion.

History can't even deny the role that the moon can play on us. The word "lunatic" comes from many different languages that reference hysteria or madness. From the Latin word "lunaticus," that originally referenced to madness and epilepsy because they thought diseases were caused by the moon; and from the Old English "monseoc," "lunatic" actually translates to "moon-sick."

Pliny the Elder, the Roman historian and Aristotle, the Greek philosopher thought that since our brains are an organ that is "moist" that our minds could be influenced by the moon's pull just like the tides.

Ujjwal Chakraborty states in his paper, **Effects of Different Phases of the Lunar Month on Humans** that many studies have concluded there is an association between the lunar phases and human reproduction, patterns of physical activity, diseases, physical health, and mental health.

Elizabeth Palermo found a similarity between the words "month" and "moon" aren't a coincidence.

Every phase of the moon: last quarter, full, first quarter, and new; everyone happens one time every month. Speaking scientifically, these phases happen due to the distance between the moon and sun and how much light gets reflected onto the moon from the Earth.

It takes the moon about 29 and a half days to orbit the Earth and during this full orbit, we can see every phase of the moon. Every phase happens about 7.4 days apart.

There are very unique spiritual meaning and energies behinds every phase. Science is able to explain some of them. The others are where faith, experience, and belief have to take over.

Living their life according to the lunar phases have always had special meanings to women since we are physically and emotionally following these same phases. When the moon has to renew, withdraw, and recede every month, we have to, too.

We travel across various emotional states the exact same way the moon orbits the Earth. The more in tune we are to the phases and the way they affect us; we can learn to harness those energies instead of wasting our energy trying to fight them.

New Beginnings – New Moon

Spiritually: New moon is representative of a woman's menstrual cycle and throughout history, women lived away from other people during this time.

Don't think about the new moon as a fresh start but a time to retreat. During this time, you can start over and renew your strength. Clean slates, fresh starts, and new beginnings surround the new moon. You need to use this time to "reboot".

Imagine your "battery" getting recharged under the new moon's energy. Throw all your unwanted junk and thoughts away.

In order to do this, you have to unplug yourself and take some time alone. You might begin to feel introverted and anti-social. Watch for these feelings and just embrace them.

When the moon turns her dark side toward us, turn away from other people's draining energy and turn inward. Never feel bad if you have to cancel plans, you don't want to answer phone calls, or be around other people.

Turning off and tuning out is the best way to make it through a new moon.

Scientifically: The new moon begins when the moon and sun are both on the exact same side of the Earth. Since the sun isn't facing the moon, from our view on Earth, it looks as if the moon's dark side is facing us.

Setting Intentions – Waxing Crescent

Spiritually: This phase of the moon brings wishes, hopes, and intentions. Once you have recharged yourself under the new moon, your desires and intentions have been planted.

This is the time you need to develop your intentions, lay the groundwork for your next project, write checks to the Universe, and bury crystals.

Scientifically: When the moon begins to move closer to the sun it begins to get lighter. You will be able to see a crescent, less than half the moon will be lit until it begins to get bigger or waxes into the first quarter.

Action – First Quarter Moon

Spiritually: Since the first quarter moon happens one week after the new moon, this is the time that we begin to feel resistance from obstacles. If you planted intentions during the new moon, you will experience your first hurdles here. Actions, decisions, and challenges will all be faced during this time.

Your time of setting intentions and rest is finished and now you have to work harder. Get ready to have to make decisions quickly and don't lose your temper if things pop out of nowhere at you.

The easiest way to hand the moon is learning to be flexible. Keep your intention you set during the new moon on your mind the whole time. Make sure the decisions you make will bring the outcome to your intentions.

The best way to begin acting on them is to keep a journal. You need to physically write and act on your intentions. Create a daily list of things you need to do and mark them off as you finish them.

Scientifically: The moon will reach its first quarter one week after the new moon. We call this the first quarter because the moon is one-quarter of the way through the monthly phase.

Refine – Waxing Gibbous

Spiritually: Editing, refining, and adjustment surround the moon during this time. Things won't always work out the way we might have wanted to and this moon phase might help you see what you need to change directions on, give up on, or reevaluate.

If you would like to reap all the benefits of the full moon, you might need to sacrifice some things. You might need to change your course. Never resist the feelings of change during this phase.

Scientifically: The waxing moon is just one phase from turning into a full moon. This moon can be easily seen in the daytime since there is a huge portion that is lit up.

Harvest – Full Moon

Spiritually: Since the moon and sun are on opposite sides of the Earth, they are also in completely opposite zodiac signs, too. This can bring more tension because we are fighting to find a balance between these extremes.

Emotions will run high during this time. It is very important not to get extremely attached or emotional to anything during this time.

The first full moon during September is called the Harvest Moon.

This is the time that farmers will harvest their crops. Just like they are reaping the benefits of the seeds they planted earlier in the year, you need to be reaping all the benefits from your intentions that you set during the new moon.

You might see these benefits show up as results from all the hard work you've done. They might show up as new opportunities, too. Be sure that you are open and prepared to receive them.

Scientifically: A full moon will happen when the moon and sun are on opposite sides of the Earth. Since the sun is sitting directly across from the moon, the light is lighting it up completely. This makes the moon look full when you see it from the Earth.

Grateful – Waning Gibbous

Spiritually: Enthusiasm, sharing, and gratitude surround the moon during this phase. You should feel all the benefits of the hard work you've done in the past two weeks. Your "crops" are abundant, and you should see some, even if they are small, outcomes from your intentions and goals you have set.

Now is the time you will be feeling full of love. You want to give back to the people around you.

You might treat your partner to a night out on the town. You might buy your friend a present just because you saw something, and it reminded you of them.

You might find yourself spending more money this week than you normally do. Don't go overboard on your spending but don't feel bad about what you have spent on the people you love. Giving back is the main theme during this phase.

Scientifically: Once the full moon has passed, the moon begins to be less lit again. It wanes toward the last quarter moon and then back to another new moon.

Release – Last Quarter

Spiritually: Forgiveness, letting go, and release surround the moon during this phase. Just like the moon is slowly getting smaller, you need to be ready to get rid of stuff. During the month you might have been angered, broken, or hurt.

During this phase of the moon is when you can release all this anger and grudges. You have to purge yourself in order to receive the intentions you will be set during the next new moon.

A good practice during this phase is cleansing. Clean out your closets, look at friendships, and clean out your house. Look for anything that isn't serving you and toss it out.

Watch out for unnecessary physical and emotional clutter that you might have accumulated during the past phases and get rid of it. In order to get rid of all this unnecessary emotional baggage, do whatever physical activity that you enjoy.

Scientifically: This phase of the moon is the complete reverse of the first quarter as it makes its way to another new moon. After a full moon, the moon will wane and get smaller. It turns into another gibbous moon, and then into the last quarter.

Surrender – Waning Crescent

Spiritually: Recuperate, rest, and surrender. You might feel completely drained during this time. You have lived through a whole moon cycle and things have happened.

You might have let things go and received things. You might have willingly received or let things go or you might have fought some things. You need to prepare for a new moon and a new cycle and there isn't anything wrong with setting new intentions but not during this phase.

Right now, you need to surrender to the Universe and relax. Some things are always going to be out of your control and fate has to have its way.

Scientifically: The last bit of moon that is lit up is getting smaller and it is on the way to be a new moon.

Chapter 5 Moon magic of the lunar cycle from new moon to full moon and back

Since the primary stirrings of human progress, the Moon has assumed a significant job in the fantasies and practices of societies around the globe. For ages, it filled in as both a wellspring of light and a method for estimating time. Like its partner, the Sun, it has been connected with numerous divine beings and goddesses around the world. In both fantasy and magic, this heavenly body has been all around related with numerous focal worries of human presence, for example, love, enthusiasm, richness, secret, demise and resurrection, and the afterlife. Today, the Moon is as yet a fundamental nearness in Wicca and different types of current Witchcraft and Paganism. Generally, Wiccan covens meet for Full Moon customs to respect the Goddess on the Esbats, a practice received by solitaries also.

THE POWER OF THE MOON

Researchers realize that the Earth has its energy, which is free from the energy it gets from the Sun. The Moon additionally transmits energy that is unobtrusive yet particular. In contrast to the Sun's manly, projective energy, lunar energy is ladylike and open. This is the energy of the Goddess. This power has frequently been portrayed as attractive, which bodes well to any individual who has felt "pulled" somehow or another by the Moon. Some especially delicate individuals feel a physical pull in their bodies at the Full or New Moon, while others see an elevated feeling of attention to everything in their condition.

Lunar energy is customized for cooperating with the energy of possessing instinct, which is additionally female, responsive, and attractive. Otherwise called the intuition, this is the most urgent method of observation when it comes to magic. So, when we intentionally associate with the energy of the Moon, we are opening up a pathway, or channel, for that energy to help manifest wanted changes in lives. Furthermore, when we do this in cognizant agreement with the vivacious rhythms of the Moon's cycle, we can amplify the intensity of the magical work. This is because each stage of the lunar period offers specific energies that can be saddled for specific magical objectives.

WORKING WITH THE LUNAR CYCLE

The connection between magic and the Moon can be comprehensively portrayed as a cycle of waxing and melting away. As the Moon develops, we work magic for increment; as it melts away, we work magic for diminishing. So, when you're looking to bring something into your life, you work with the waxing Moon, and when you need to exile or discharge some undesirable component of your life, you work during the melting away phase.

The transitional point between these two contrary energies is the Full Moon, a time of "reap" as we celebrate what we have manifested over the principal half of the cycle. We then basically "tidy up" a short time later, identifying and discharging what is never again required during the time half of the cycle. At the New Moon, we set new expectations for the following round of manifestation, without any end in sight it goes. The musicality of this cycle can be envisioned as the cadence of the tides, which the Moon is causing.

Here are some broad recommendations for timing your magic with the phases of the Moon:

New Moon: This is the earliest reference point of the lunar cycle and a decent time for longing for what you wish to make in your life. Customarily, magic planned for starting new tasks and adventures is favored as of now. However, anything, including pulling in or expanding what you want is fitting.

Waxing Moon: This phase is the perfect time for making a move toward the objectives—really starting, on the physical plane, the activities we've expected for on the profound plane. The energy here is one of activity and anticipating the goals outward into the Universe. Magical work might be related to picking up or reinforcing organizations with others (regardless of whether they be companions, sentimental interests, or business relates) and improving physical wellbeing and general prosperity.

Full Moon: This is the most dominant phase of the whole lunar cycle. Numerous Witches find that the day of the Full Moon is the most magically intense day of the month, and may spare spellwork related to especially significant objectives for this event. Any magical objects are favored during a Full Moon custom.

Melting away Moon: This is the time to discharge the energy of outward activity and line up with the energy of internal reflection. Wiping out negative energies and encounters is the prevalent magical objective now, so spellwork planned for beating deterrents, settling clashes, and evacuating reasons for an ailment is fitting.

Dark Moon: In the days just prior to the New Moon, numerous Witches shun effectively working magic, picking instead invigorate their energy for the following waxing phase.

Be that as it may, innumerable others observe the Dark Moon to be the best time for magic related to the conclusion, or bringing things full circle. There is a damaging potential to the energy now that can be saddled for discharging any karmic designs that harvest up over and over in your life, for example, those related to need, surrender, betrayal, and so forth.

CHECK OUT THE MOON FOR ENHANCED MAGIC

Relatively few individuals who are new to magic have been in the propensity for giving everyday consideration to the rhythms of the Moon's circle around the Earth. If this incorporates you, consider embracing a practice of associating with the Moon every day, regardless of whether through a formal custom or only a concise, quiet welcome.

Discover where the Moon is in its cycle and recognize this as a major aspect of your everyday practice—you can discover the Full Moon plan on the web. This will enable you to adjust to the unpretentious differences in lunar energy from the stage to stage. From New to Full, to Dark and turn to New again, the ceaseless cycle of the Moon presents numerous chances to tune into the energies of the common world and improve your spellwork.

A WICCAN GUIDE TO MAGIC AND THE LAW OF ATTRACTION:

Over the previous decade, an ever-increasing number of individuals have gotten comfortable with the expression "Law of Attraction," as books, motion pictures, and classes about this subject have been grabbing the eye of a regularly developing group of spectators.

Be that as it may, the Law of Attraction isn't only an ongoing wonder. It has been talked about by journalists and masterminds from different profound, philosophical, and mysterious foundations for a few centuries, including numerous professionals of magic. You could state that for Witches, this general fundamental rule is intrinsic to all spellwork, regardless of whether the spell caster acknowledges it or not!

WHAT IS THE LAW OF ATTRACTION?

This standard is regularly summed up as "like pulls in like," or "thoughts become things." It's a method for clarifying that the Universe reacts to your thoughts and feelings, carrying your conditions that line up with your predominant vibrational recurrence, which is dictated by your convictions about what is conceivable. For instance, have you seen that if you choose to accept that no doubt about it "awful day," encounters that match, this conviction will keep on appearing throughout the day? However, if you center during the day around positive thoughts and emotions, you will pull in positive encounters.

Numerous individuals battle with this idea, as it infers that everything that has ever transpired—regardless of whether positive or negative—is their very own consequence thoughts and convictions. This is presumably the greatest obstacle to move beyond when it comes to placing the Law of Attraction into purposeful practice in your life. For sure, there's significantly more to it than the genuinely oversimplified expression "thoughts become things" would recommend, and an exhaustive comprehension of how it truly works is past the extent of only one thought. In any case, you don't need to get a handle in general picture to make the guideline itself work for you. What's more, if you have an enthusiasm for the magical expressions, you're now well on your approach to deliberately using the Law of Attraction!

MIND GAMES: SHIFTING YOUR ATTITUDE

If you generally read about the Law of Attraction, you'll locate a differing cluster of activities and methods for shifting your thoughts and convictions to pull in what you want into your life. A large portion of these methodologies will, in general, be established in at least one of three critical devices: thankfulness, affirmation, and perception. While each is valuable all alone, it's the blend of the three that genuinely enables your brain to roll out the required improvements.

Thankfulness, likewise frequently alluded to as appreciation, is attention on what is going admirably for you, regardless of whether you're concentrating on the prompt present minute, or on your life when all is said in done. When we try posting and perceiving the positive in lives—and see the positive emotions that outcome from this center—we are consequently shifting the consideration away from the negative, placing ourselves in a spot to draw in a more significant amount of what we appreciate.

Affirmation is the demonstration of rehashing positive explanations, regardless of whether quietly or so anyone can hear, that portray the truth we're hoping to make. For instance, if you need to expand your budgetary prosperity, you may make an affirmation like this: "you have all that you need and more for a safe, copious life." If you're looking for a relationship, you may state, "you are in a sound, the adoring relationship, you're your ideal match." Affirmation requires an eagerness to "counterfeit it till you make it" by imagining that you have just manifested your objectives. It can feel somewhat senseless from the outset, yet numerous individuals have discovered that through rehashed practice, after some time, their affirmations do turn into their world.

Representation, as you may expect, is the practice of making mental photos of the conditions we want. You invest energy envisioning the house you need to live in, the fantasy occupation you're chasing, or the condition of wellbeing you're hoping to accomplish. The objective of perception is to make a striking feeling you had always wanted working out as expected, yet it includes something other than having the option to see it in your imagination—you likewise need to make the sentiment of having accomplished your craving, because this is the thing that truly starts the way toward transforming your thoughts into things.

A MAGICAL ALIGNMENT

For the Witch, it does not shock anyone that these equivalent three procedures are worked in parts of magic. Most spellwork includes a blend of gratefulness, affirmation, and representation, working together in a synergistic manner that takes into account the ideal manifestation to come through on the physical plane. Perception of the ideal result of a spell is vital to centering your goal, and valuing the result—ahead of time—is a piece of the intensity of the representation. Affirmation is the verbally expressed piece of magic, the words that whole up and "send" the activity of the work—regardless of whether you're lighting a flame, charging an apparatus, or making a charm. As you express the expressions of a spell, you are "doing what needs to be done" that you've set up by imagining and valuing the possible result.

Magic has regularly been characterized as the utilization of centered aim to realize an ideal impact, regardless of whether that impact is a deluge of cash, another relationship, an improved living circumstance, or something less unmistakable, similar to a clearer comprehension of a current issue. The individuals who work purposefully with the Law of Attraction are doing precisely the same thing. However, they might be utilizing spellwork to "help" their advancement. An accomplished Witch's comprehension of magic is considerably more perplexing than the fundamental aphorism of "thoughts become things"— there are other basic standards at work in the Universe that go further in lighting up how and why magic works. In any case, the Law of Attraction is undoubtedly part of the more significant framework, and once you have a reasonable handle of "like pulls in like," your magic will undoubtedly turn out to be increasingly viable.

THE WICCAN "BRILLIANT RULE"

Liquid as Wiccan magical practices might be, notwithstanding, there is as yet the one fundamental "rule" to remember consistently: Harm None. Taken from the Wiccan rede, this straightforward expression reminds us to be mindful to look at the thought processes and intentions when picking or making a spell.

We're not originating from a spiritual spot if we wish to work the magic that would carry adverse outcomes to someone else, period. Be that as it may, "hurt none" additionally applies to any manipulative magic, regardless of how good-natured we maybe about it. This implies we don't work magic to influence the emotions or conduct of anybody other than ourselves. We likewise don't work magic for others without their unequivocal authorization, and we never attempt to choose for others what their best advantages are.

Chapter 6 What Do Wiccans Believes

The Horned God / The Sun God

The masculine god is often seen or referred to as the horned god. Horns are a traditional symbol of masculinity, representing qualities such as strength, sex drive, and energy.

During the Wiccan year, the horned god will adopt different personalities. For half of the year he can be referred to as the Oak King and for the other half, the Holly King. He is also referred to as the Sun God who is worshipped on the Sabbat of Lughnasadh. Some Wiccans believe that these are all different gods and will worship each of them separately and other Wiccans have them all fall under the God.

The Goddess / The Triple Goddess

The Goddess is the Feminine deity. Like the horns represent the masculine god, the Goddess is represented by three phases of the moon. This is why she is also called the Triple Goddess. Each phase of the moon represents a different form of the Goddess. The waxing moon represents creation and inspiration, the full moon represents sustenance and the waning moon represents fulfillment. The three forms of the Goddess are as follows:

The Maiden - The maiden is young, full of beauty and innocence. Her future is promising and filled with potential. She is associated with beginnings and the new moon. The Mother - The mother is experienced and mature. She is protective, nurturing and selfless.

The Crone - The crone is full of wisdom, a leader and respected. She reminds us of our mortality and that our bodies will one day return to the earth. Despite this, she does not have a negative connotation. In fact, she is seen as a guide and her wisdom can help us through difficult times.

The Wheel of the Year

The Wheel of the Year is the Wiccan calendar if you will. It represents the annual cycle of the Earth and is derived from the seasons. Wiccans believe that time is cyclical, a continuous cycle. This is why the festivals (or Sabbats) are represented by a wheel.

The wheel also represents the progression of life. We are born, we grow, we live, we decline and then we die. This period of birth, life, and death is represented by the life of the Horned God during different seasons. The cycle of fertility (virginity, pregnancy, and birth) is represented in different seasons by the Triple Goddess.

The Sabbats

Yule: December 20-23. Yule is the winter solstice. The Goddess (in the form of the mother) gives birth to the sun god.

Imbolc: February 2. Candles are used to celebrate this Sabbat. They are to encourage the sun to shine brighter. The sun god at this stage is an infant and feeds from the breast of his mother, the Goddess. This also represents the end of winter because the earth is starting to feel the warmth of the infant sun.

Ostara: March 20-23. The spring equinox. The God is now a child, and the Goddess will take on the form of the maiden. She acts as the God's playmate and they play in the fields to encourage the flowers to bloom.

Here is where beginner Wiccans might get confused. The Goddess has now taken on two forms simultaneously. She is both the playmate of the child God (as a maiden) and the nurturing (mother) of the child. She will continue the year changing from two forms as needed in order to serve the life cycle of the God.

Beltane: May 1. The Maiden Goddess and the Sun God are now young adults. They are fertile and ready to procreate. For this reason, Beltane is viewed by Wiccans as a sacred night for sex. Fertility also represents the upcoming crops. The Sun God will impregnate the maiden here and she will turn from the maiden to the pregnant mother. The Goddess is now both the pregnant lover of the God as well as his nurturing mother.

Litha: June 20-23. The summer solstice. Litha is the peak of the Sun God's life, he is now full of strength and masculinity. Litha is when the Sun God and the pregnant Goddess will get married.

Lughnasadh: August 1. Autumn is upon the earth. The leaves are turning brown and the temperature is cooling. The Sun God is dying. The God will begin preparations for his death and make sure that his unborn child and the pregnant Goddess are taken care of. The Sun God knows that winter is upon the earth and it will be a challenge to survive it. He knows that his strength and light can only be renewed if he willingly offers himself up as a sacrifice. He will do this to become one with the earth to provide sustenance. His sacrifice will be the wheat that is harvested for the winter.

Mabon: September 20-23. Time with the Sun God has nearly ended. Preparation for his death and the winter are in full swing. Knowing of losing her son, the nurturing mother transitions into the crone. Her wisdom and experience will help guide us through the mourning of the Sun God.

Samhain: October 31. The Sun God dies. Many Wiccans believe that this is when the Sun God is referred to as the Horn God. He is animal-like, he is one with the earth.

During Samhain, the crone and the pregnant mother goddess mourn the God's death. Samhain is the start of the New Year for Wiccans and many Wiccans view Samhain as the most important Sabbat. Samhain is a day to remember those who have passed on, including ancestors, family and even animals that were either pets or used on a farm. Samhain rituals celebrate darkness.

Although it is considered the beginning of the year, it also marks the end of the previous year in which rituals celebrate and commemorate last year's harvest and the accomplishments that were made.

Samhain also represents a promise of new life. The pregnant mother holds the seed of the reincarnated Son God who will be born at Yule.

Yule: December 20-23. The Goddess gives birth and the Sun God is reborn, thus re-starting the cycle.

The Greater Sabbats and the Lesser Sabbats

The eight Sabbats are divided in half making four of them greater Sabbats and the other four, lesser Sabbats. The divide is as follows:

Greater Sabbats:

Samhain (October 31)

Imbolc (February 2)

Beltane (May 1)

Lughnasadh (August 1)

Lesser Sabbats:

Yule (December 20-23)

Ostara (March 20-23)

Litha (June 20-23)

Mabon (September 20-23)

The four lesser Sabbats mark the end of one season and the beginning of the next while the four greater Sabbats are the middle or the peak of the season. These days are considered days of power.

Esbats

Although the Goddess plays a key role in each of the Sabbats, they are mostly used to outline the life cycle of the God or the sun. The Goddess is represented by the moon, as she is the polar opposite of the God. Therefore, we celebrate the Goddess during **Esbats** which follow the phases of the moon rather than the sun.

As a reminder, the Triple Goddess is represented by three phases of the moon. The maiden is represented by the waxing moon, the mother by the full moon and the crone by the waning moon. Esbats take place whenever the moon is full, which means they occur twelve or thirteen times a year.

The Blue Moon Esbat

During each solar year, there will be either twelve or thirteen full moons. The thirteenth full moon (or Esbat) will occur once every two and a half years and this is referred to as the "blue moon". This Esbat is rare and is considered to have more power and energy than a regular Esbat. The presence of the Goddess during the blue moon is very powerful and is a great time for beginner witches or Wiccans to establish a connection with her. The blue moon is a time that Wiccans find very sacred and they will hold special rituals under the light of the blue moon.

My First Blue Moon Ritual

The first time I held my own blue moon ritual was truly astounding. See, as a Christian, I had never had a spiritual experience with a feminine deity. Since I am a woman, I always felt that side of my spiritual being was missing from my religious faith.

I went outside to perform my ritual under the moonlight and called upon the Goddess, hoping that I would be able to feel her presence. Although I couldn't feel her right away, a few minutes (or maybe an hour?) in and I knew she was there with me. I could feel her telling me that I was not lesser or weaker because I was not a man. Without her power, the God would not exist and I felt myself understanding my role as a woman on this earth. Motherhood, fertility and nurturing kindness were all equally as important as strength, the need to provide and masculinity. If you are a woman, I highly recommend taking part in a ritual under the full moon. You will feel an overwhelming sense of belonging and understanding of your place on this earth. If you are a man, I recommend performing this ritual even more. See masculine and feminine energy aren't limited to one gender or the other. There is a feminine side to you and if you have grown up Christian, that side of your being has likely been ignored for years. Making time to appreciate the Goddess and how her feminine energy lives inside you will help make you truly whole. At least that is my theory on the matter, every Wiccan is free to take their own path.

Reincarnation

Unlike Christians, Wiccans do not believe in the idea of heaven and hell but we do believe in an afterlife, or a place where the soul can live without the physical body.

As a witch on this earth, your purpose is to better yourself, better your environment and help others. You are to go through life's ups and downs, learn from your mistakes, collect wisdom and grow as a person. This is the same purpose that your soul has.

Your soul is meant to experience the physical world, die, reflect on the life it lived and then be reincarnated into a new physical life. The goal is that each physical life is lived better than the last. For this reason, we can assume that people who are immoral and treat others badly are "new souls" who have not yet lived many lives and learned how to be good.

The Afterlife

Every time your soul lives a life and reflects upon it in The Afterlife, it will live a more moral and spiritually satisfying physical life the next time it is reincarnated. It's like your soul is on a mission to live the perfect physical life and it takes numerous tries for this to happen.

So, what is the Afterlife? The Afterlife is a place (similar to the idea of heaven) where your soul can go and rest before it is reincarnated into a new physical body. Unlike heaven, however, this place is not a place where your soul will be judged. While you are in The Afterlife, you can communicate with the other souls, the deities and reflect on the physical life you just lived. If you lived a bad life, you will follow the guidance of the Goddess and the God in hopes that your next life will be more spiritually satisfying. Once your soul has satisfied the physical life's purpose, it will remain in The Afterlife for all eternity.

The God and Goddess (or Lord and Lady)

Wicca acknowledges both the masculine god and the feminine goddess. They both represent unique but essential characteristics and are seen as equal. Now for Christians, the deities in Wicca can be confusing, I know it was for me! This is because Christianity focuses on a very rigid set of beliefs but Wiccans have the ability to interpret things on their own. Some Wiccans view the God and Goddess as two gods. Other Wiccans believe there are many different masculine deities which collectively would be referred to as the God or Horned God and that there would also be many feminine deities that all together would be referred to as the Goddess or Triple Goddess. To compare this to Christianity, we can use God, Jesus, and the Holy Spirit. In Christianity you would consider all three of those entities to be "God" but they can either be broken down into individual entities or referred to as a whole.

In Wicca, you have the ability to choose whether you want to refer to the God and Goddess as a whole or if you'd like to worship the individual deities and break them down further. I will outline the basic overview of the God and Goddess but I recommend delving deeper into this on your own.

Other Beliefs

The Rule of Three

The rule of Threefold means that whatever energies we put into the universe, it will be returned to us times three. This can include every day acts of kindness or negativity or a lifetime of treating people or a person in a certain way. Wiccans who do not practice magick or witchcraft still abide by the rule by the actions they choose to do and the decisions they make every day of their lives.

For Wiccans who **do** practice witchcraft, this rule becomes even more significant. Once you are able to create spells and harness your powers, you will be able to cause things to happen to people. You can use this power for good or bad but the Threefold rule states that whatever we put out into the world; it will come back to us threefold so mind what you do as it will come back to you.

The Elements

The elements are integral parts of Wicca. The elements: earth, wind, water, and fire are seen as the components that make up the earth as well as energies that make up living beings. This means that they are considered the root of all matter. The elements are often a large part of rituals and are used in their physical forms to purify a ritual circle.

Fire:

Fire is an integral part of a comfortable human existence but we do not necessarily need it to survive. Fire gives us warmth in the cold, allows us to cook food and is a source of light in the darkness. For these reasons we should look to fire less as a survival element and more of a luxury in which we should offer our deepest gratitude. Fire is also one of the more dangerous elements and should always be treated with caution and respect.

Fire is used in candle magic and also to create an environment for rituals and spellwork. In rituals, fire is represented in the form of burning objects, baking and lighting candles or bonfires.

Symbol:

Deity: The Sun God

Energy: Masculine (to will)

Tools: Candles, bonfire

Season: **Summer**

Corresponding Zodiac Signs: **Aries, Leo, Sagittarius**

Air:

Air is a symbol of our intelligence and our ability to communicate with other humans on this earth as well as the spirits. Air is how some Wiccans have psychic powers and telepathy.

Unlike fire, air is crucial to our survival and reminds us of the importance of being connected with both earthly beings as well as spiritual beings. It reminds that we are very fragile and we can be transferred to the afterlife if we are without air for only a few minutes.

Air is used in rituals by tossing objects into the wind, burning incense of aromatic candles. Air is used in spells that involve freedom, knowledge, traveling and psychic powers.

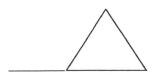

Symbol:

Deity: The Sun God

Energy: Masculine (to will)

Tools: Wand, incense, bell

Season: **Spring**

Corresponding Zodiac Signs: **Gemini, Libra, Aquarius**

Water:

Water is the most versatile of the elements. It can be present in the form of a liquid, solid and gas and each of those states can be used to excerpt different magical qualities of water. Water is an integral part of our lives and is used to nourish ourselves as well as the earth in the form of plants and animals.

Water is a symbol of the subconscious, purification, wisdom and emotions. It is the element of love and femininity. In rituals, water is represented by pouring water over objects, making brews, and ritual bathing.

Symbol:

Deity: The Triple Goddess

Energy: Feminine (to listen)

Tools: Cauldron, cups

Season: Autumn

Corresponding Zodiac Signs: **Pisces, Cancer, Scorpio**

Earth:

Earth is the foundation upon which all is built. As Wiccans, we take pride in our relationship with the earth and consider the earth a direct pathway to the divine. The more we take care of our earth, the more we honor the God and Goddess. The earth is a symbol of life. All life is born of the earth, grows and is nourished by the earth and then returns to the earth in death. The earth represents strength, abundance, prosperity, and femininity. In rituals, the earth is represented by salt, burying items in the ground, herbalism and crystals.

Symbol:

Deity: The Triple Goddess

Energy: Feminine (to listen)

Tools: Pentacle, a bowl of salt

Season: Winter

Corresponding Zodiac Signs: **Taurus, Virgo, Capricorn**

Wiccan Symbols

Just like Christians have the cross, Wiccans also have symbols that represent different aspects of the faith. Although there are many, I will cover the four main ones below.

Pentacle:

The pentacle is a pentagram within a circle. It is the most common and traditional symbol of Wicca.

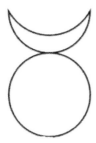

The Horned God:

This symbol represents the masculine God as we can see his horns above his body. The horned God is also known as the Sun God.

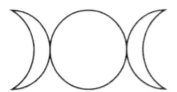

The Triple Goddess:

This symbol represents the Triple Goddess with the phases of the moon representing each of her forms.

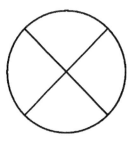

Wheel:

This symbol represents the wheel of the year, and a cyclical view of time rather than linear. Each piece represents one of the eight Sabbats.

Chapter 7 Life-Changing Moon Manifesting Visualization Strategy

After you have a clear intention set and you've got your mind, body, soul and environment on board, you will used advanced, but easy visualizations to enhance the energy of the goal.

Using visualization techniques and repeating powerful affirmations, along with the energy of the moon- we supercharge our dreams and wishes at an even more accelerated rate!

If you can see it in your mind, you can hold it in your hand. Visualization is comparable to a super power! When using the moon to crush your goals, we will use science based, strategic visualizations to trick your brain and bring these goals into fruition quickly!

When it comes to our visualizations two things are important- First, we must fast forward in our mind, and imagine ourselves living in the moment as if the goal were already true. We want to visualize how the situation looks once we have attained the goal!

So, if your goal is to have more self-worth, you will imagine and visualize yourself going to the gym every day, raising your hand in a meeting with confidence, or seeing yourself eating healthy and taking care of yourself.

If you want to manifest a promotion- you will visualize yourself having a meeting with your boss, hearing the great news, moving into your new office, and imagine your pay increase by visualizing massive deposits coming to your bank account!

Do you get it? Your goal is to make your intention as real as possible in your mind. The more detail you can picture the better! You can even write this visualization down and hang it, or place it next to your intention paper.

The second most important part of visualization is feeling the feelings and emotions your intention will bring you. How will it feel when you're self-worth is back? How will it feel when you've finally gotten the promotion you've been working so hard for? It's going to feel damn good! So, the last part of our visualization we FEEL!

You will picture yourself feeling proud that with your promotion you can finally afford to take your family on vacation. You will feel happy that financial stress has been removed from your life. You will feel your confidence build and feel feelings of joy that your self-worth is back!

It doesn't matter what your goal may be- you really want to get deep into the feelings and emotions that will come with this newly attained goal.

So now that you've set your intention, have a good visualization of that intention, and have brainstormed on all the feelings that intention will bring with it- you're ready to put everything together and complete your Moon Manifesting Visualization exercise.

90 second Moon Manifesting Visualization

Sit or lay down in a quiet space.

Close your eyes.

Take a few deep breaths and release any tension in the body.

Picture a funnel at the top of your head and imagine a white light pouring through it, and into your body.

Imagine this light filling your entire body from head to toe, covering every part of your body until every cell is illuminated. Image this light is swirling within you and around you, as if you're floating in a white bubble of powerful energy.

Picture yourself walking down an illuminated path that is leading you to your intention or goal

Arrive at a real-life scenario where you've obtained the goal.

How does this goal look? What are you doing? Who are you with? What can you see, taste, smell and touch? Make this goal as real as possible in your mind- visualizing as many aspects as you can.

Visualize the moment you receive your intention.

How does this intention FEEL? How does it feel to have it? Run through at least 3 feelings and emotions. Smile and make it as real as possible!

Show gratitude and appreciation for this vision and affirm that you know it will be true for you at the perfect time.

Float back to earth enriched by your vision.

Lock in the feeling of power, and know that you are in control of your life, and you have the power to make this happen!

You are going to do this exercise for 90 seconds every morning, and 90 seconds every night before going to bed. The most effective time to visualize is first thing in the morning and right before bed, so of course, you are going to do just that!

You dream deserve 180 seconds per day! This exercise will not only help you attain your goal- it will uplift your spirit, set a positive tone for your day and help you sleep better at night!

Crafting Your Master Plan

Next, we must make a strategic plan that will lead us closer to our intention.

What can we bring in, or let go of in order to be totally ready to receive this intention? How serious are you about this goal? For goals to bloom they must first start with intention, and planning is the next extremely important factor.

What steps can you take to set up your environment? What small actions can you take immediately, and what big actions can you already sense will be necessary? Think about all of the things you may have to do now, and start immediately.

Create your plan the last night of the new moon or the first night of the waxing moon. Remember, each phase has 3 days.

In this phase, we don't have to exactly know *how* we are going to get there- but we have to plan out *some* milestones in order for the goal to be fully attained. Don't worry about every step, you will be guided once you start taking action.

For example, if your dream is to get a promotion, and you have only thought and visualized about it, but haven't planned or set yourself up for success- the goal will not align.

You are a magnet, you are constantly attracting and bringing different situations into your life. If you want a promotion, you've got to set the intention, visualize on it and then you must make a plan to speak with your supervisor about it. Set a date, decide what you will say to your boss and plant the seed in your bosses' mind that you're interested.

A second part of your plan could look like gathering all your latest work to show your boss at that meeting, and then schedule a follow-up to seal the deal a few weeks down the road.

An important note to remember, your plan needs to align with the energy of the moon and her phases. Your worst-case scenario would be setting a date to meet with your Supervisor to show you are the candidate for that new high paying position on the Balsamic Moon when energy is null.

Set the date during the New or Waxing phase, and catch your boss when the energy is momentous. When you start planning and scheduling important dates with the moon- your life will transform in ways you did not think were possible.

All of the fine details will work themselves out, doors will start opening and leading you to your goal, but you have got to plan the essential stepping stones you know need to happen to make this baby work!

Planning is essential for any goal to manifest. Plan out a few steps you can take right now and get started right away!

Pro tip: When it comes to manifesting- don't worry about the little details, just focus on the end goal working out perfectly and the steps you need to take to get there. When you take action on your plan, time it with the moon and trust that the energy from the universe is helping you- nothing can stop it from manifesting!

Waxing Moon: Taking Action

Next, we must act on our plans. We must start showing the moon and the universe that we mean business! The energy during the waxing moon is momentous, forward moving and energetic.

These two weeks are a busy time, and really the only two weeks of the month you have to take strategic action.

After setting the intention, visualizing the shit out of it, and crafting your plan- you have to take massive action.

I wish it was so easy, we could set our intention, say a few affirmations, and wallah- it's here! But, unfortunately, this is not how the universe works people. We have to act in order to receive.

We have to show intent and act upon that intent for this system to truly work. Start taking small steps and use this phase to your advantage. The sooner you act, the sooner you shall receive.

Remember to continue practicing your moon manifesting visualization every morning, and every night. The universe works in laws and by visualizing every day, you are using the law of attraction to attract your goal to you rapidly.

Full Moon: Gratitude & Release

The full moon is where we pause, reflect and have a moment of gratitude for how far we've come. WOW, We're doing it. We're making changes, doing the work and each day we are getting closer!

For some of you, you may have never dug this deep into a goal. So, it's time to be thankful and pat yourself on the back.

During the full moon everything is illuminated the good, the bad, the bittersweet, and the ugly. The energy during the full moon asks us not only to be grateful, but to become aware of what isn't working, and release it from lives for good.

It may be part of the plan that needs to go, or it may be a toxic person holding you back, or even an old belief that keeps you stuck. Whatever it is- thank it for what it was worth and let that shit go!

If you are serious about your moon manifesting mission- you must let go and create space for your new manifestation. If toxic people or toxic thoughts are holding you back, the universe will not deliver.

Let go. Release it forever. Say good-bye. You are blooming into the person you want to become and you have no time for heavy energy holding you down.

I recommend performing a Full Moon ritual, taking a bath and sitting outside under the full moon and releasing what needs to go under this energy.

Waning Moon: Reflect & Revamp the Plan

The two weeks of the waning moon, energy is decreasing, slow moving and can almost feel overwhelming, chaotic and confusing. Remember, this is not the time we are beginning ANYTHING new.

These are two weeks we are analyzing the plan- tweaking and changing what we can to do more, to do better on the next moon cycle. In this phase we are looking deep into ourselves, tuning in, and allowing the universe to guide us. Our goal is to stay in tune with the flow and energy of the moon and universe.

You need to really become aware during this phase. Become aware of your thoughts, your feelings and make sure your goal still aligns with your vibe and purpose.

You need to become aware of what's working and what isn't. So many times, we hold onto things in our lives that weren't meant for us. If your plan feels hard or uninteresting, maybe it isn't for you!

More often than not, people find that what they thought they wanted, wasn't for them, and things change. If this is the case for you- that is okay! Move on and start anew, with a new goal, on the next new moon.

On the other side- You may be feeling more passionate about your goal then ever! Signs and synchronities may have already started appearing in your life, or some of you may already be living your dream.

Wherever you are is perfect. You just need to reflect, weed out the weeds and water the flowers now during the waning moon.

Balsamic Moon: Treat Yo' Self

Balsamic actually comes from the word *"balsam"* which means to soothe or relax, and this is exactly what this phase is all about. The balsamic, or dark moon phase is the last phase of the cycle and the energy is asking us to let go of all worry, and pause our actions, and to just melt into total relaxation.

These three days where we are in total chill, no f*cks, no stress type of mood! These are three days of the month where total self-love and self-care is first priority!

Some people may find these three days very tough, as most of us do not put ourselves first or set time aside for self-love each month. Others may wish this phase was longer. However, you feel- you should schedule a solo soothing activity or plan to veg out at home.

Take a bubble bath, infuse it with essential oils and crystals, light some candles and let your body, mind and soul totally let go. Get a massage, acupuncture, go on a meditation retreat, or take a walk in nature. Allow yourself to be free from your phone and "reality" as much as you can during this phase.

When we give ourselves space from our goal and slow down for a moment, we allow a re-set to happen on a subconscious level. When we begin again on the new moon, we will feel energized, recharged and motivated to keep going.

Life is all about balance, and if you really want to achieve your goals, you have to relax. If you keep going and going, you will get totally burnt out! This is why we must take a break, each cycle, each moon, each month.

Rinse & Repeat

You made it through your first moon cycle and first intention cycle!!! Pat yourself on the back and be proud- you are aligning and becoming one with the abundance of the universe. You may have already attained your goal in just one cycle, but for most of us this won't be the case.

As I said earlier, where ever you are is perfect. When the next new moon arrives, it's go time! You've revised your plan; you've taken a break and It's time to jump back into action.

Start fresh each new moon and repeat this step by step strategy until you make it happen! Your goals may take time to manifest, the universe will only deliver when you are totally ready. You have to be ready in your inner world, your other world, and have unshakeable faith that your dream will come true for you!

It's essential you follow all of the steps in this book, accordingly. If you do not visualize, if you do not set a clear intention with a clear plan, and if you do not take action- there is no way it's going to happen!

A dream is just a dream without action, faith and imagination. If you dream big, work hard and believe in yourself- anything is possible.

Chapter 8 Candle Magic Guide

Different colored candles are used for different spells because of their meanings. When you look at a yellow color, you feel happy, and when you think of the color green you usually associate it with nature or money. The same concept is applied to candles and their colors. Each color has a different vibration and frequency which matches different spells.

For example, blue is associated with meditation, calmness within the body and healing of fevers, cuts, and bruises. Since the blue's properties match the vibrations of the blue candle, you can't expect to heal a fever with the yellow candle that has a completely different vibration.

When spell casting, it is important you first determine your goal and what spell you are casting before choosing the correct candle. Each candle is also associated with a specific day of the week which can aid in enhancing the power of the spell, energy, and intentions. Now, although, if you cast a spell on a different day than stated, it still has a pretty good chance to work out, it is recommended you cast a spell on it's said day below unless the spell instructions state otherwise. It is important for the spell to activate its full power and with good intentions, it can succeed.

Black candles can help fight evil. They have a strong power to banish negativity, a person, or spirits from your life. These candles do not represent bad luck, instead, they are associated with universe's healing energy, forgiveness and moving on from different situations, and it can help leave behind old troubles. Cast spells on a Saturday, during a waning Moon if using this candle.

White candles represent purity, protection, white magic, and blessings. This is also the only candle that can be used to substitute any other candle in spells. It is mostly used in spells regarding a change, marriage, birth, cleansing, healing emotionally, and peace. The white candle represents the Moon, and spells using this candle should be cast on Monday.

Purple candles are associated with enhancing psychic powers, intuition, and your vision through your third eye chakra. It can cancel out bad luck or bad karma within a person or yourself. The purple candle can aid in accessing knowledge or wisdom regarding the higher realms, and the usage this candle should be cast on a Thursday. Physically, this candle can cure allergies and colds.

Blue candles are the most spiritual and healing candles. It can help clear mental fog, doubts, or uncertainty, and bring peace and harmony to the mind. This is a spiritual candle, anything involving your higher self, astral travel, meditation, or any spiritual troubles should use this candle on a Thursday. Physically the blue candles can heal almost anything from fevers, bruises, cuts, blood pressure, headaches, woman problems, and insomnia.

Green candles are associated with money, good fortune, nature, financial affairs, and good luck. It is a rich candle, and not just in terms of money. If casting spells regarding marriage, add the green candle to enhance love and provide good luck. Involving green candles, cast the spell on a Friday. Physically, the green candle can heal colds, woman problems, and headaches.

Red candles represent love, passion, and lust. They are mostly used when casting spells relating to romance, soulmates, or sexual desires. The red candle can also be used for purification, bravery, courage, and inspiration. This candle represents strong emotions and should be cast on a Tuesday.

Yellow candles symbolize the mind, creativity, focus, inspiration, visualization, and memory. Often, this candle is used to help pass a test and invoke memory. It can also represent good luck, happiness, prosperity, and can be used in divination work. The yellow candles should be used on a Wednesday. Physically, this candle can cure indigestion and diabetes.

Orange candles are the action energy needed to achieve goals. This candle can help with sexual attraction, creativity, enthusiasm, sex magic, good luck, gaining control, courage, and weight loss. Anything involving the law or business is associated with the orange candle. Casting such spells should be done on a Sunday, in the middle of the day when the sun is strong. Orange candles can also help heal depression.

Pink candles are the purer version of the red candles. Instead of passionate romance, this candle can help attract your other half into your life. It's an innocent color involving friendships, stability, purification, self-love, travel, and new beginnings. If you are looking for a change, then this candle is for you. Pink candles should be used on a Friday. Physically, pink candles can help heal anxiety and depression.

Silver candles are associated with the Moon goddess. It represents mental clarity, awareness, astral realm, intuition, insight, and can help communicate with spirits and ancestors. This color is also connected with love, psychic abilities, healing, and dream magic. This candle should be burned on a Monday.

Gold candles can help you answer questions, or guide you on your destined path. They also represent protection, good fortune, skills, success, and security. The color gold itself represents money and wealth and casting spells on a Sunday with a gold candle can help you attract money and financial success into your life.

Brown candles are associated with nature, grounding yourself, earth magic, stability, nurturing, balance, and healing. It can aid in communicating with nature and animals. Brown candles represent the Mother Earth and when connecting to the element of earth, you should use this candle to strengthen the connection. Cast spells using this candle on a Monday, Friday, or Saturday.

Candle colors are just one layer of candle magic. Essential oils, herbs, and sigils are other layers that are not necessary but can help enhance the power of the spells and the intentions.

Sigils

Sigils should be carved first before applying any essential oils. Sigils are powerful symbols or signs that can enhance the spell. For example, if you are casting a spell on protection, you will need a protection sigil, carved into the candle. You can always just carve the word itself, but sigils can enhance the intentions. There are many different and popular sigils online, below are some of the most basic and common sigils for different spells and rituals.

△ Air	♉ God	⚼ Money	Ƶ Cause sleep
⚔ Deadly	)O(Goddess	⚴ Mother	◎ Spirituality
⚲ Blessing	⚶ Health	⚬⚬ Peace	♅ Spring
⚹ Crone	⚹ Lose weight	⛤ Pentacle	∪ Summer
∪ Deosil	♡ Love	☆ Pentagram	┼ Travel
⊕ Earth	⊘ Magick circle	△ Protect child	▽ Water
♏ Fall	❋ Magick energy	⚛ Protection	∩ Widdershins
◊ Fertility	✿ Magick strength	⚱ Pyshic awareness	Ⓜ Winter
△ Fire	⚸ Maiden	◊ Purification	⊠ Witch
◊◊ Friendship	⚭ Marriage	◎ Rebirth	◊ Yonic

You can always make your own sigil and design it however you seem fit, this gives it more energy and charges it. Sigils can also be written on a piece of paper, drawn in notebooks, or even sewed on pillowcases to promote a good night's rest. Once you've finished carving it, activate it by placing your hands on the candle, or whatever you put the sigil on, visualize yourself feeling protected, for example, if that was your sigil, and simply connect your energy through your fingers and to the sigil.

Essential Oils

There are so many different essential oils and each of them has a different and unique ability. Essential oils are just another layer used to cleanse and charge the candle in order to purify it and give it all the necessary energy to carry out your intentions into the world. Below are some of the basic essential oils for candles and what they are used for.

Love - **Cyclamen, Rose, Gardenia, and Jasmin oils**

Concentration - **Honeysuckle, Rosemary, and Lilac oils**

Fertility - **Musk and Vervain oils**

Protection - **Cypress, Rose, Rosemary, and Geranium oils**
Courage - **Iris, and Musk oils**
Meditation - **Hyacinth, Magnolia, Acacia, and Jasmine oils**
Harmony - **Gardenia, Basil, and Lilac oils**
Money - **Mint, Vervain, Honeysuckle, and Bayberry oil**
Healing - **Sandalwood, Myrrh, Rosemary, and Lotus oils**

There are also two main ways to properly dress a candle with essential oil. Put some oil on the tip of your fingers, not too much. If you want to attract something into your life such as love, money, or luck, you have to rub the candle downward, from the top to the middle of the candle while setting your intentions. If you wish to abolish or banish something from your life, then rub the candle in a downward motion, from the middle to the bottom. Remember to never rub a candle back and forth, it can cancel out any intentions that you are setting.

Herbs

Herbs are another layer which is often added after applying essential oil onto the candle and just like essential oils, each is used for a different purpose. Below are a few of the main herbs used on candles that can be found in your kitchen.

Basil is used for love, business success, peace, happiness, and money. Physically, it can heal a headache, reduce anxiety, act as an antibiotic, and even prevent flatulence.

Chili powder is used in spells to ward off unwanted or negative energies or boost the energy of the spell. Physically, it can act as an antioxidant and help reduce fat.

Cloves are used to stop gossip, promote strong protection from evil and promote wealth. Physically, it can help reduce toothache pain, inflammation, and even an aphrodisiac.

Black pepper is used for banishing, binding, exorcism, and protection from unwanted or negative energy. Physically, it can help heal from the flu or a cold and can aid in digestion.

Cinnamon can deliver fast money, wealth, healing, happiness, and love. Physically, it can reduce stress and prevent car sickness.

Rosemary is used for healing, blessing, love, and purification. Physically, it can help relieve a sore throat.

Salt is the most common herb which can help purify, cleanse or heal the body, mind, and soul. Physically, it can help reduce sinus swelling.

Tips and Tricks

Always remember that a white candle can be used to substitute any candles and, in any spells, because it absorbs all the colors, but reflects none.

Always cleanse and clean your candles when you get them from a store. Candles are known to pick up other vibrations from different objects or people, and you never know if those vibrations are good or bad. Always remember to cleanse your candles when you first bring them into your home and before you start casting spells. Candles should not be blown out, that often is like an insult to the element of fire. You can always use your wet finger to put out the flame, or if you are too scared then a toll can help. Simply covering the candle and cutting out its oxygen can also help put it out but be careful to not burn anything down.

It is not necessary, but during spell work, many practitioners let their candles be burned down all the way to ensure that the wish has been heard loud and clear through the smoke of the candle.

When you attempt to light the candle and for some reason, it doesn't light up, it means that right now is not the right time to be casting this spell. You are either not mentally ready or there is something going on around you, some unknown force is trying to stop you or help you. In this case, carefully think through what could be the problem or the solution.

When the candle goes out during your spell work, it can also mean that something is interfering with your work. If it's a negative energy interfering, then you should immediately cast a protection spell and banish it.

Beeswax candles are known to be the most powerful candles.

You can always make your own candles from a couple of ingredients while doing so, the candles catch on to your positive vibrations which helps unite the energy when casting spells.

When looking or gazing into the candle flame, you can strengthen and focus your intentions. It can also be used as a substitute for meditation if you are in a rush.

Different colored candles have different purposes, if you use the wrong colored candle for a spell then you can get completely different results from what you asked for or in another scenario, the spell can backfire on you and make everything worse. Follow instructions of the spell carefully to see which color to use or if you are casting your own spell, take some time to determine which candle would suit the spell best.

Chapter 9 The months of the year and the days of the week, correlations with the moon

A s you continue to delve deeper into understanding Wicca, you will learn about covens and circles and the difference between them and solitary practice. You will also discover that it is quite tasking to directly access other Wicca practitioners. This is because there is no central place of worship where, as a beginner, you can go to seek insight and guidance.

"Coven" is a Latin word that means to "meet up." It was widely used during the Middle Ages to describe social gatherings of different types. In the early 1600s, covens were more associated with witches. Covens gained further popularity in the mid-20th century as the "Old Religion" was being re-introduced.

A coven was initially a 13-member of witches who secretly met to practice. A coven was comprised of a High Priest and a High Priestess who spoke to the God and the Goddess. Today, however, covens do not necessarily have to have 13 members. Different Wiccans were initiated into the tradition following either the belief systems of Alex Sanders or Gerald Gardner. Some Wiccan covens will follow the initial traditions while others embrace different varied beliefs.

Most Wiccan covens have a set-out tradition of initiating new members into the coven. These set-out traditions are custom and the coven requires the new members to fully invest themselves in the initiation. Once the new member is initiated, other requirements follow to ascertain the new member's commitment to the coven. There are different levels of initiation and the new members follow certain custom conditions to get from the first to the third degree. The prerequisites to progress from one degree to another are dependent on the coven a member is following.

As a common practice, a Wiccan coven will mark the Sabbats and Esbats celebrations. Others will also mark other days between these two celebrations. For these celebrations, if a coven intends to include a new member, then they will invest their time and energy into getting the individual ready. Members of the same coven are family to one another. The members have a very close bond. Therefore, when a coven intends to welcome a new individual, all the members are invested in the process including the individual in question.

If you are a beginner in Wicca, it is highly unlikely that you will immediately join a coven. This is because most covens require one to have been practicing for more than a year especially before you can go through the initiation process. This is a great requirement because it ensures that the individual is fully certain and committed to being part of a Wiccan coven. Understandably so, if joining a coven is difficult for you, you might consider finding other practicing Wiccans within your locale and joining their circle or you could simply start your own circle.

A circle is a gathering of individuals who are Wiccan practitioners. They meet to talk and explore the Craft. It could conceivably include a normal Sabbat and additionally Esbat celebration. However, on the off chance that these occasions are marked, participation is common but not compulsory.

Contingent upon the general inclinations of the gathering, there might be numerous individuals, some of whom drop in and out as it suits them, or only a couple of consistently included companions. The structure of a circle is commonly free and doesn't require official inception or include a setup chain of importance. Amateurs are regularly welcome, and you're probably going to locate a wide scope of information and experience levels around, where everybody contributes their very own point of view.

If you can't locate any similarly invested people in your general vicinity, don't be concerned. There are numerous online networks of Wiccans and different Witches to study, and there are likewise numerous advantages to solo practice. Actually, by far most of the Wiccans in the 21st century are solo practitioners. Becoming more acquainted with the otherworldly and mystical parts of the Universe all alone can be extremely fulfilling!

In case you're sure you need to work with others, be that as it may, you can approach the Goddess and God to attract the opportune individuals to you. At that point be tolerant, trust divine planning, and your coven or circle will, in the end, show up in your life.

As a solo practitioner, we can explore how you can initiate and dedicate yourself to the practice. A custom of self-commitment may look like parts of a coven initiation to changing degrees, but since single Witches can structure and play out this custom in any capacity they like, it is on a very basic level diverse experience.

Self-dedication happens entirely without having to conform to anyone else terms. The dedication you're announcing in such a custom is true to your internal identity, or to any gods you may join into your training, and to the heavenliness of the Universe as you comprehend it. It is anything but a promise to some other individual, or passage into a gathering of individual experts. What's more, since this experience is entirely among you and the universe, you can consider it whatever you like—initiation, self-commitment, self-initiation, or something different completely, if that is the thing that sounds good to you.

In spite of the fact that this is an altogether different ordeal from that of a coven initiation, there are still critical parallels on the adventure to this achievement nonetheless. In the first place, obviously, is crafted by truly figuring out the Craft—investigating conceivable roads as far as learning customs, getting a sense of what impacts you and what doesn't, and proceeding to seek information to any extent you feel applicable and as broadly as possible. It's generally prescribed to go through a year and multi-day contemplating the Craft before attempted your self-initiation, yet you can positively take longer on the off chance that you understand the process.

When you feel prepared to step toward initiation, you can begin contemplating what this will mean to you.

In case you find yourself interested, you can take parts of one practice and other parts from another, making up your own way toward Wicca practice. Yet, you can at present concentrate on learning as you work your way toward the point where you feel prepared for initiation. You can "allocate" yourself a specific measure of study every week and arrange your investigations around explicit themes. For example, the Triple Goddess or the Wheel of the Year, and additionally peruse every one of the books composed by a specific writer before proceeding onward to another one. On the other hand, you might find that you are interested in a diversity of books, following your intuition so that you are able to grasp from these books the information you feel is relevant to you.

With regards to the Wiccan initiation custom itself, you can structure your own process of initiation. Simply realize that the subtleties are less critical than your genuine want to formalize your pledge to the Wiccan lifestyle. You can even ask the Goddess and God to enable you to pick your best method.

Self-dedication is an individual choice that nobody can make for you, except if you are looking for enrollment in a coven. It's really a completely discretionary thing. In any case, regardless of where you look for initiation, realize that a solitary custom won't abruptly launch you into an out and out mystical presence, or certification that you'll remain on this specific route for eternity. There are Witches who have worked for their entire lives without experiencing initiation, and a lot of beginners who lost enthusiasm for Wicca did not follow through. For a long time during the initial phases, it will be dependent upon you to keep choosing your way, in your own particular manner and at your very own pace.

Wicca is regularly thought of as an approximately organized or even totally unstructured custom which is quite deep and for some individuals who were brought up in progressively formal composed religions, this is certainly part of the charm. In any case, there is a central component of Wicca that serves to unite individuals around an aggregate center, which is made up of Wiccan customs.

Regardless of whether the event is a Sabbat, an Esbat or an achievement, for example, a handfasting (wedding), an inception, or an end of-life service, covens and circle individuals will accumulate to share their love and respect of the Goddess and God, and commend the initiation to be found in the continuous cycles of life. While most Wiccan ceremonies are held in private, a few covens will once in a while hold theirs out in the open, with the goal that all who wish to watch can come and get familiar with the Craft. Numerous Wiccan circles do likewise, and may even welcome general society to take an interest.

Obviously, solo ceremonies are no less noteworthy, and singular Wiccans realize that as they venerate at each point along the Wheel of the Year, they are including their own light and capacity to the group otherworldly energy on these exceptional events.

Beautiful and mysterious, Wiccan ceremonies can take various structure, with no two occasions being actually similar. Some might be very organized and elaborate. This is frequently the situation with coven ceremonies. However, since most covens keep the subtleties of their customs secret - known only by initiated individuals - it's hard to portray them with much precision. Different ceremonies, especially those by single and varied Wiccans, might be genuinely basic by comparison, and may even be made up on the spur of the moment.

The substance of some random Wiccan custom will rely upon the event. For instance, Esbats, or Full Moon festivities, are centered exclusively upon the Goddess, while Sabbats respect the co-inventive connection between the Goddess and the God. In spite of all the conceivable varieties, nonetheless, there are a couple of essential components that will, in general, be incorporated into what we may call an "ordinary" custom.

To start with, there is decontamination, both of the celebrant(s) and where the custom is held. This can occur as a custom shower, as well as a smirching service to expel any undesirable energies from the custom space, regardless of whether it's an outside region or inside the home. Smearing includes the consuming of consecrated herbs, for example, sage, rosemary or lavender.

Setting up the altar happens first. A few Wiccans can keep a raised area permanently set up in their homes. However, even in this situation, it will probably be enriched contrastingly relying upon the event, for example, getting fall foliage for Mabon (the Autumn Equinox) or Samhain (otherwise called Halloween.) The special stepped area is part of the different Wiccan customs and will be decorated in accordance with the event that is being celebrated.

Next comes the casting of the circle, an action that sets a limit between the spiritual realm and the mundane physical world. The altar is normally the focal point of the circle, with a lot of space for all required to work unreservedly inside the circle, with no incidental venturing outside of the boundary, which is thought to contain energy. The circle might be set apart with ocean salt in a long line, a few stones, herbs or candles. There are numerous techniques for circle-casting that you will discover for yourself as you practice.

When the circle is cast, the ritual starts. The invocations here can change, yet ordinarily the God and Goddess are invited to join the ritual and afterward, the four Elements—Earth, Air, Fire, and Water—are summoned (In numerous customs, a fifth Element—Akasha, or Spirit—is additionally brought in.) In different conventions, this invocation, known as calling the Quarters, and the four bearings (North, East, South and West), is tended to, either rather than or notwithstanding the Elements.

When these actions have occurred, the core of the celebration starts. To begin with, the aim of the ceremony is expressed—

regardless of whether it's to praise a Sabbat or an Esbat, or maybe to pray to the God and Goddess for the benefit of somebody who needs it or some other sort of help.

After the intention is expressed, the fundamental body of the custom may comprise of different exercises. The point of convergence might be the execution of a custom dramatization. For example, reenacting scenes from antiquated legends or sonnets—or other ritualistic material, contingent upon the convention of Wicca the gathering is following. Single Wiccans may likewise peruse from old enchanted messages, or make their very own verse for the event. Reciting, singing, moving as well as other ceremonial motions might form a part of the ceremony, and the season in which the ceremony is held will have great significance. Supplications may be offered, regardless of whether they are close to home or for the benefit of others. Truth be told, it's regular in a few conventions to use customs to encompass not only thoughts of those within the coven, but also for those outside of it.

In numerous celebrations, a service known as "cakes and brew" (or "cakes and wine") is an imperative part of Wiccan history. Sustenance and drink are offered and emblematically imparted to the God and Goddess, ordinarily toward the end of the ritual.

Wicca: book(s) of shadows

A Book of Shadows is fairly similar to a diary, however with an unequivocally otherworldly and supernatural core interest. It might incorporate spells, names, and dates of Sabbats and Esbats, mantras and other custom dialect, arrangements of enchanted correspondences for hues, precious stones, and herbs, and a large group of another valuable supernatural randomness.

The Book of Shadows is basically a cutting-edge grimoire—a term utilized in the nineteenth century to portray writings covering different Witchcraft activities, for example, enchanted hypothesis, portrayals of ceremonies, guidance in spell work and divination frameworks, magical rationalities, and other exclusive data. Instances of grimoires can be found all through the Middle Ages and much prior, at least going back to stone tablets found in old Egypt and Mesopotamia.

It was Gerald Gardner who received the expression "Book of Shadows" as a title for his very own coven's grimoire, which was intended to be kept a mystery from everyone except the chosen individuals from his coven. The material was added to and updated as time went on, with the understanding that these practices ought not to wind up static and settled, but rather ought to rather stay dynamic, with new ages of Witches including and subtracting from them as they saw fit.

As Witchcraft developed into Wicca, it moved into new and different customs gaining new insight adding to the making of new Book(s) of Shadows – However, not all Wiccans keep a Book(s) of Shadows to record their mystical knowledge and magical experiences. Most covens that abide by the old Wicca traditions keep their mystical knowledge and magical experiences a mystery.

Despite the fact that it is unexpected for a Wiccan to completely share with others their Book of Shadows, it is for that reason that knowledge about it has come into the public domain and gained interest from people. In the current day of the Internet, some Wiccan practitioners actually share their Book of Shadows online. Therefore, the mystery that surrounds Wicca continues to diminish. However, it is important to note that it is quite standard for Wiccans to conceal their Book of Shadows from other people who might not understand the Craft.

The elements and grounding techniques

Wiccans believe that everything, essentially, comes down to the four elements of earth, air, fire, and water. These elements make up the world, the universe, and ourselves. This connection between us and the elements of the universe is the backbone of Wiccan magick and the theory of how it works.

There is a story not of Wiccan but of Taoist origins which represents this perfectly.

The story tells of an old man who was walking by a river when, suddenly, they lost their balance and fell into the rushing waters. An onlooker, concerned that the old man would drown, sent his proteges to go save the man. But, by the time they reached him, the old man had already washed up on the side of the river and seemed to be undeterred.

When asked how he was able to escape the raging waters, the old man explained that he escaped them by not fighting them. Fighting them meant that he was separate from the river. Instead, he allowed the river to carry him and he became the river. In so doing, he was freed.

Magic has often been labeled as 'supernatural' but Wiccans believe their form of Magick is perfectly natural. They are simply working with nature rather than fighting against it and, in doing so, are able to work what to others may seem like miracles.

To harmonize with the elements and make magick possible, there are a few grounding techniques. However, before we get to them, you can also learn to harmonize with the four elements by trying to adopt their properties into your everyday life.

Earth represents fertility and stability. You can learn to adopt the traits of the Earth by allowing the things you do in life to grow and blossom without having the need to control. And, you can stabilize yourself by learning how to create within you an inner calm and choosing to help people in times you would rather stay far away.

Because fertility takes trust, you must learn to trust the universe. And, because stability requires self-reliance, and it welcomes the people in harder times to seek you out. Let them know you are there for them and your stability with shine, like the rock solid stability of the Earth shines.

Air is connected to the center of your essence but also to the nature of the world. It represents the lightness of your inner spirit but also the winds of change which bring both good and bad things and yet do not have prejudice against them.

You can learn to adopt these traits by being playful and becoming less attached to the world as you know it. These traits come in unison. The inability to be playful stems from taking life too seriously and taking life too seriously is how we try to control the uncontrollable world around us. By loosening up, having fun, and letting life take you where it will, you are welcoming the aspects of air into your being.

Fire is related to vast energy and strong power of will. You can incorporate these traits by dividing your energy more wisely and by staying firm on the things you believe in. In order to do either of these, you must know yourself better than you do currently.

We waste so much time on the things that do not matter and on the trivial. When we choose instead to devote our time and energy to the things important to us, almost limitless energy is born. And, with that energy, we can stay steady and firm on the things we believe in. We can push through the hard days and be a formidable force.

Fire can both create and destroy, so use the energy and willpower it grows within you to do great good, because nothing burns worse than the fire of the universe coming back to haunt you later on. Know yourself and stand strong, but have mercy.

Water is associated with cleansing, passion, and emotion. But the passion represented by water is not a burning passion, but a steady passion. Like the waves which work away at the rock slow and steady, never ceasing, rather than the TNT that could blow the rock away.

In order to allow these traits into your being, you must start with cleansing. By far, the most unclean part of ourselves is the mirror through which we view ourselves. The opinions of others and happenings of the past cloud our opinion of ourselves and often make us increasingly arrogant or devastatingly insecure – both of which are really the same issue expressing themselves in different ways.

To cleanse your inner mirror, you must learn to forgive yourself and let go of the past. Once you have done this, you will see the person you truly are and you will be able to see the clouded images others present – and you will be able to assist them to love themselves as well.

To express the passion of water, you must remain steady and consistent. Passion is not the explosion followed by the silence, but it is the constant working away at your goals. Set something up in your life that seems difficult and work away at it steadily – soon you will know the passion of water.

And, lastly, there is emotion. A word which carries a negative connotation for most people because they rarely see it expressed in any way other than in a burst. So many of us hold in our emotions that, by the time we have a chance to be sad we are devastated or depression, by the time we have a chance to be angry we go on rages or become destructive, by the time we have a chance to express joy it becomes utter mania.

To align with the emotional side of water and allow yourself to harmonize with nature, you must learn to acknowledge what you are feeling and begin to experience emotions in the same way you would experience smells and tastes. You cannot deny them, can you? They certainly are there, you cannot ignore them. But the only time a smell becomes pungent is when the cause has been allowed to fester. Do not allow your emotions to fester, allow them to flow – like water.

When you have become aligned with these elements in the ways outlined, it may not even be necessary to become grounded because you will already be in harmony with the world and the universe. But, until then, grounding will be the only way you can truly take part in magickal practice. Any magickal practice.

Quick Grounding Technique

For quick grounding, you can simple relax yourself in an environment where you are not going to be interrupted. Take slow breaths and try to become aware of what is around you. This works especially well in nature, where you can specifically focus on the earth, air, fire, or water elements depending on your surroundings. The idea is to slow down your mind and body and to reconnect with the world around you. This can be done at any time. It begins when you choose and it ends when you feel stable and relaxed.

Deep Grounding Technique

For deep grounding, you will want to envision far more and settle yourself deep within the visualization. What exactly you envision depends on the technique, but the following is an example:

Place your feet flat on the earth (bare if possible) and keep your back straight. Relax your mind, relax your body. Breath slow.

Now, imagine the earth beneath your feet. Envision the layers of soil or flooring beneath you, way, way down. The further down you can see the better. Then, imagine a golden snake of energy slithering up through the layers, one by one, until finally it enters through your feet.

Feel the golden energy spread down to your toes and then up your legs, your back and fill up your stomach. Imagine it shining on your heart and passing into your arms and neck. And finally, feel the golden light's warmth as it spreads through your face and up through the crown of your head. Imagine the golden snake reaching high to the sky.

Focus on the warmth and the stillness of your being for a few moments before reversing direction, slowly, from the sky down through your body, out of your feet and back down deep in the Earth. Imagine the golden light leaving you gradually from head to toe.

You have now been grounded, thoroughly, and may continue on with magickal practice or with the rest of your day.

Chapter 10 Simple Spells and Rituals

- Casting a Circle

A magickal circle is multifunctional. It carves out sacred space, keeps wanted energy in, and keeps unwanted energy out. Sacred space is traditionally a place between worlds and dimensions. It's a section of time and space that does not belong to the mundane, nor is it completely etheric. It is where magickal rites and rituals are performed: "a time that is not a time and place that is not a place; between the worlds and beyond". It serves a temple that can be erected anywhere.

As a beginner, it's advisable to cast a circle prior to all forms of magickal practice and worship. Simply casting a circle to sit and meditate or to bond with the God and Goddess is perfectly acceptable. Practicing magick is of course just that—a practice. Witches and Magicians are practitioners of magick just as doctors are practitioners of medicine. The only way to become adept is through practice and experience.

The more times you cast a circle, the more familiar you will become with the ritual and with your own ritual mindset. Getting to know yourself in the circle is one the most effective forms of refining your Craft. Eventually, some Witches find that casting a circle is only necessary when performing major magickal workings, while others may continue to cast a circle before all spiritual work including their morning meditation.

The best advice is to do what feels right for you. There is no "wrong way" in Wicca. It's all about finding what works best for you as an individual—this is how your magick becomes effective. Trial and error are necessary within a magickal practice

With that in mind, note that the following steps are only guidelines. This is one of the simplest ways to cast a circle. Some methods are more formal, and require several other steps. Feel free to omit, modify, or add whatever resonates with you and makes you feel the most comfortable.

1. Cleanse and Purify the Ritual Space

Traditionally, the room or area is cleaned. Physically cleaning begins the process of clearing out any stale or negative energy. If you're inside, this means picking up strewn items, sweeping or vacuuming, etc. If you're outside, clear away branches and debris. In some Wiccan traditions, the floors and walls are always scrubbed before casting a circle. If you're a solitary eclectic practitioner, you can take the cleaning as far as is comfortable for you personally.

If you're in a place that doesn't allow for this step, that's fine as well. However, you definitely want to energetically cleanse the space. Smudging with sage, sprinkling salt water, fanning incense around the area, playing a musical instrument or singing bowls will neutralize the environment. You can simultaneously visualize a white light filling the room and pushing out any negativity that may be present.

2. Set Up

An altar is ideally located in the middle of the room, facing either north or east. Again, if this is impractical, you can still cast a circle with your altar against a wall or in corner through visualization. The idea is for your altar or working space to be in the middle of the circle.

- Make sure you have everything you'll need for the spellwork. Once the circle is cast, if you need to leave the circle for any reason, "cutting" a door with your athame or wand is customary.

113

- Lay out your altar cloth and arrange your tools.

- Determine how large your circle needs to be to accommodate the type of work you will performing. Most solitary practitioners can work comfortably in circle with a six-foot radius. Others may require less or more.

- If possible, mark the ground to visibly show where your circle will be. This could be done by laying a rope or cord of some kind in a circle, a chalk outline, a ring of salt, flowers laid stem to petals, or simply four candles placed at the cardinal points of your circle. If you're working up against walls, you can visualize the boundaries of the circle through the wall.

- Light your working candles.

3. Cast the Circle

There are a number of ways to do this. The simplest way is as follows:

- Begin by standing at the north end of your circle's outline with athame or wand in hand. If you're using only your hand, extend your pointer and middle finger to assist in the projection of your energy.

- Point your tool towards the ground where your circle will begin, and visualize a stiff beam of protective energy being directed into the ground. This energy is coming from you, and is only being directed into the ground by the athame or wand.

- Walk clockwise (also known as "deosil") around your circle, while continuing to project the beam of protective energy into the ground. The stronger your visualization, the stronger your circle will be. Take your time, and don't rush through the casting.

- Once you return to the north, your circle is complete.

4. Grounding and Centering

Once your circle is cast, take a few moments to sit at your altar space and take several deep breaths. Light some incense of your choice, and meditate for however long it takes to enter a ritual mindset. Commune with the God and Goddess. Invite any deities to come and witness your rites. You will notice a shift in your consciousness. When you do, it's time to begin your magickal work.

5. Perform Any Magickal Work

After casting the circle and entering the ritual mindset, it's time to perform your spell, or complete whatever magickal task you set out to accomplish.

6. Close the Circle

When you've cast your spell or otherwise completed your magickal work, you might want to stand up and thank the Goddess and God for attending. After doing so, you can begin closing the circle.

- Stand at the north point of the circle with your athame, wand, or fingers pointed toward the ground.

- Visualize the beam of protective energy retracting back up into you.

- Walk counterclockwise (also known as "widdershins") around the circle, while continuing to visualize the beam being retracted.

- Once you reach north, the circle is closed.

7. "Cakes and Ale"

After all your spiritual work is complete, you may want to sip and nibble on some treats to reintroduce yourself to the mundane world.

Simple Candle Spell to Manifest Love

This spell can be adapted to manifest love of all kinds. Simply alter the color of the candle, the herbs and oils used (if any), and the intention to reflect what you want to attract.

1.   Define Your Intention

First, there must be an intention. What would you like to accomplish with the spell? As an example, let's say you'd like to work on self-love and invite a loving relationship with yourself. From what we've already learned, we know that this is a form of creation magick—you want to bring something in.

What would this intention look and feel like to you? Imagine yourself bubbling with happiness, feeling loved and accepted. Maybe imagine yourself having a conversation with someone else and feeling confident. Keep this image in your mind and really feel the emotions associated with it throughout the entire spellcasting process.

2.   Timing: Determine When to Cast the Spell

Choosing when to cast is dependent on each individual spell. Since this spell is going to invite self-love into your life, you would want to work with the Goddess and attune your spell to the waxing phase of the moon (the full moon would also promote this and all other spells).

To clarify how we came to this conclusion of when to cast, let's say you are casting a spell to smoothly end a relationship with someone else instead. Rather than cast the spell during the waxing phase of the moon when the energy is best suited for building, the waning phase would be more appropriate since the waning moon represents ebbing or subsiding.

Timing a spell can include many more factors: the day of the week, month of the year, and the astrological placement of other planets. However, as a beginner, timing your simple candle magick spell with the corresponding phase of the moon is a great way to start.

3. Select a Candle: Color and Size

Next, you will need to choose a candle best-suited to your intention. Below you will find a list of colors and their correspondences. For this example, spell, you are inviting self-love into your life, so you may feel drawn to use either a pink candle or a red candle. Traditionally, pink symbolizes a soft, sentimental love—charming and sweet.

In addition to self-love, pink is also commonly used for friendships, familial connections, healing, femininity, and the more romantic aspects of a lover-to-lover relationship. However, if red feels more like love to you, or if any other color better symbolizes the type of love you're wanting to attract, please use that color. In spellwork there are only guidelines. The most potent spells are custom-made.

In addition to the color of the candle, the shape and size are also dependent on the individual spell. Generally, votive and tapers are sufficient for almost any spell. You will find that votive and tapers are readily available in an assortment of colors. Large, seven-day candles are appropriate for more intensive work, as these will burn continuously for a week. For our sample spell, a pink votive or taper would be ideal.

Below is a list of the most commonly used colors and some of their correspondences. These will vary depending on the Witch. Follow your intuition. For example, if a gold candle feels more like prosperity to you than a green candle, then use a gold candle for your prosperity work.

- White

White candles can be used in place of any other color. If you need a pink candle but only have white on hand, the white candle will do just fine. As you may know, this logic comes from the field of physics. It has been scientifically observed that white is all colors. What we see as white is actually all the wavelengths of visible light at once—all the colors in the spectrum.

Common correspondences of white include: healing, protection, the Goddess, purity, enlightenment, etc.

- Black

Just as white is all colors, black is the absence of color.
Correspondences: banishing, reversals, protection, pure potential, the blank canvas.

- Green

Many thinks of the lush, fertile Earth during spring and summer.
Correspondences: the element of Earth, the heart chakra. abundance, prosperity, money, career, the material world, etc.

- Pink

Correspondences: romance, self-love, friendship, partnerships, the planet Venus, femininity, etc.

- Red
- Correspondences: the element of fire, the root chakra, passion, lust, desire, ambition, courage, strength, power, renewal, transformation etc.

- *Purple or Violet*

Correspondences: the element of spirit, clairvoyance, psychic abilities, meditation, third eye, wisdom, spiritual protection, etc.

- Blue

Correspondences: the element of water, the throat chakra, calming, healing, truth, justice, etc.

- Orange

Correspondences: the element of fire, the root chakra, cleansing, refreshing, motivation, ambition, optimism, activity, warmth, welcoming, etc.

- Yellow

Correspondences: the element of air, the solar plexus chakra, clarity, sunlight, cheery, communication, words, sound, intellect, logic, etc.

- Brown

Correspondences: the element of earth, stability, domestic life, animals/pets, material goods, physical health, etc.

4. Cast a Circle (optional)

The previous three steps were preparation. Now is the time to cast your circle, if you feel compelled to do so, and begin your work.

5. Dress the Candle (optional)

Many Witches feel that dressing a candle adds to the potency of the spell. Dressing a candle refers to carving letters, symbols, and/or sigils into the candle, followed by coating the candle with essential oils and herbs which resonate with the intention of the spell. In the following section titled, "Herbal Magick", you will find a list of commonly used herbs and their correspondences.

For our example spell of inviting love, you may want to dress your pink votive or taper by carving a few hearts into it, anointing it with rose oil, and rolling it in rosemary and/or jasmine. The process of dressing a candle is generally done as follows:

- Carving the Candle

Choose a symbol which is meaningful for you and corresponds to the intention of the spell. Carve the symbol into the candle where ever and however many times you see fit. You can be as elaborate and detailed as you want with the etchings, or simple and rudimentary.

In any case, be sure that you are focusing on your intention throughout the entire carving process. You can even imagine your desire being transferred into the candle through the markings. Any tools can be used for the carving—safety pin, needle, pencil, etc. Some Witches will only use their athame, and that's fine as well.

- Anointing the Candle with Oil

Apply two or three drops of the oil into the palm of your hand. Then, clutch the candle in your hand while still thinking of your intention. Massage the oil (and your intention) into the candle. Please note that if you don't have a specific oil for a spell available, like rose oil, you can always make your own in a pinch.

If you have roses nearby, take a few petals and put them in a container with some olive oil or whatever oil you have on hand. Don't be afraid to improvise when necessary. Remember, you are what makes the spell work.

- Rolling the Candle in Herbs

Once the candle is anointed with your desired oil, you will lay the candle on a bed of your chosen herbs. Since our example spell is to bring something into your life, rolling the candle toward you is fitting. Contrarily, if you were performing a spell to rid something from your life, rolling the candle away from you to coat it with herbs would be preferable.

6. Light the Candle and Raise Energy

When you feel that the candle is ready to be lit, take a few deep breaths and place the candle in a holder of your choosing. You can use a lighter, matches, whatever feels most comfortable. Take some time to sit and meditate with the flame. Soften your gaze, let your lids droop a bit. Use the flame as a focal point for visualizing your intention.

You can continue to visualize and feel the emotions of the scenes you've chosen. Additionally, chanting and swaying or rocking helps to raise the energy. You can begin by swaying back and forth slowly and gradually you will pick up speed. Chants don't have to rhyme unless you prefer them to.

If you're drawn to chanting, you can simply say whatever is in your heart to describe your intention. As an example, for this spell you might want to chant something straightforward like, "I love myself unconditionally". Alternatively, you can compose a beautiful piece of poetry to recite. Again, do what feels natural.

7. Disposal

Customarily, the candle is left to burn out on its own. The purpose of allowing the candle to self-extinguish is two-fold. Firstly, as the candle burns, it is releasing your intention and all that energy you imbued it with into the universe through the flame and the rising heat. Secondly, each time you see the candle burning, you are reminded of the spell and your intention.

This second aspect of the manifestation has a continuous impact on the subconscious mind. Meaning, you may not always consciously acknowledge your spellwork when you pass by the candle, but it does have a subconscious impact each and every time.

8. Close the Circle (optional)

If you casted a circle before beginning your work, now is the time to commence with closing.

Simple Candle Spell to Banish

This spell primarily utilizes the fire element to rid yourself of something unwanted. Fire is swift and thorough in its transformation. The results will manifest quickly, but the route of manifestation can be situationally intense.

1. Define Your Intention

What needs to be banished from your life with urgency? This could be something like a stalker, or another type of threatening presence in your life. You may want to quickly end an abusive relationship or legal situation.

2. Time Your Work

If possible, it would be ideal to wait until the time of the dark moon to perform an abrupt banishing. Perhaps the dark moon is within a few days. If not, the next most appropriate time would be during the full moon, or the waning moon.

3. Select a Candle: Color and Size

A black votive or taper candle is ideal for banishing. Black corresponds to the dark moon and the energy of renewal.

4. Cast a Circle (optional)

Cast your circle in preparation for your spellwork.

5. Write Down What You Want to Banish

On a small slip of paper, write down what you want to banish. While you're writing, be sure to focus on your intention. Visualize the situation being released and feel the emotions associated with it. Channel it all onto the slip of paper through your pen.

6. Dress the Candle (optional)
You might feel drawn to carve the candle with corresponding symbols or words. Carving what you wrote on the slip of paper works well. You can also dress your candle with the appropriate oils and herbs as detailed in the previous spell. For banishing, try anointing your candle with clove oil and coating it with crushed bay leaves by rolling it away from you.

7. Light the Candle and Burn the Slip of Paper
Light your black candle, which represents the transformative element of fire. The slip of paper is now representative of the situation or person you'd like to banish from your life. Hold the paper over the candle's flame and allow it to ignite. Once it's smoldering well, drop it into your cauldron or other fire-safe receptacle. Let it burn to ash. Continue to visualize the situation and emotions being released.

8. Close the Circle (optional)
You may want to close the circle at this time.

9. Disposal
Allow your black candle to burn down completely. The ashes can be disposed of by way of any other element. Toss them into the wind, bury them in the ground, flush them down the toilet, or throw them into a running body of water.

Create with the Earth Element: Simple Flower Spell

The element of Earth is solid, steady, and gradual in its pace. Think of how slowly but perfectly a tree grows—this **is** Earth magick. The intricacies of constructing a tree take time to complete. Thus, any intention that you cast utilizing the Earth element will manifest into your world much like the evolution of a tree. It will take ample amounts of time to flourish, but the results will be long-lasting, sturdy and well-composed. Consider manifesting with the element of Earth when your intention would most benefit from "slow and steady wins the race".

The concept of the flower spell is to charge a seed with your desire and then plant it. As the flower buds and blooms under your care, so will your desire bloom into your physical world.

1. Define Your Intention

This spell is for something you'd like to bring into your life (or generally bring into being) gradually and smoothly. It will be something you want to carefully nurture into fruition. Perhaps you are repairing a relationship with a certain individual; trust may have been breached, but you're both ready to rebuild.

This takes time and patience, which is in perfect alignment with the element of Earth. Alternatively, you may want to foster peace and bring more love to the world. Perhaps you want to become pregnant and grow a healthy child. These are all prime examples of intentions that are best manifested through the element of earth.

2. Timing

Since you are wanting to gradually cultivate something, you will want to correlate your spell with the waxing phase of the moon.

3. Charge the Seeds

You can select a specific type of seed that correlates with your intention or has some significance—rose, sunflower, carnation. Cup the seeds in your hand and concentrate on your intention. This time it will be the seeds that are representing your desire.

Focus on the emotions associated with what you want to bring forth. If you're casting this spell for fertility, visualize the healthy development of your baby within the womb, and then visualize rocking him or her in your arms. Feel the emotions as if the event is presently taking place. Visualize these emotions and images being transferred into the seeds.

4. Plant the Seeds

Once you feel that you've sufficiently raised and transferred the energy, it's time to plant the seeds. You can plant them in your backyard, directly into the earth. If this is not possible, a large pot or container filled with fertile soil is just fine. Wherever you plant the seeds, make sure they are accessible to the sun's nourishing rays.

5. Cultivate

Nurture your seeds into buds and beyond. Water them, talk to them, give them love. As your flower grows and blooms, so will your intention.

Banish with the Earth Element: Simple Apple Spell

This spell imbues an apple with something you want to banish. Then, by burying the charged apple in the ground, you rid yourself of the unwanted aspect gradually and organically.

1. Define Your Intention

You realize there is something you want to remove from your reality. Reflecting on the issue, you decide that this aspect of your life would best be dissolved gradually and delicately, rather than instantly go up in flames or get turbulently washed away in torrent. Some examples might be: gracefully ending a relationship with someone, banishing bad habits, addictions, weight, negative thought patterns, emotional blocks, hate or racism on the planet.

By invoking the element of Earth to gradually and sustainably banish these aspects, you are ensuring the durability of the results. You won't successfully crash diet, for example, and then gain all the weight back shortly after. Rather, you may start taking real steps toward a complete lifestyle change instead. The results will not be instantaneous like working with the fire element, but they will be more likely to last.

2. Time Your Work

Since you are gradually banishing, you will want to time your spell with the waning phase of the moon.

3. Cast a Circle (optional)

4. Charge the Apple

Select an apple or any other fruit with thin skin. You're going to charge the apple with your intention just as you would with a candle. Hold the apple in your hands and focus on what you want to remove from your world. Really feel all the associated emotions and transfer them to the apple. If you're wanting to banish an addiction like smoking, for example, feel that craving for nicotine, feel the guilt every time you light up, feel the burn in your throat, feel the toxins flooding your body, feel the tightness in your chest, and send all those sensations and emotions into the apple.

You'll notice that the apple now represents your addiction, just like the candle represented your desire in the candle magick spell for self-love. No matter what you're wanting to banish, the apple will become that thing once it is charged with the energy of that thing. In other words, the apple simply becomes another medium for your thoughtforms to be physically manipulated. You can get as elaborate as you'd like with charging the apple. Consider carving the apple with symbols just as you would carve a candle. Cutting the apple in half, spooning out the core, and then filling it with tobacco or cigarette butts is a more tangible way of imprinting your intention to quit smoking. You can also fill and/or dress the apple with any oils or herbs you feel are conducive. Additionally, you may want to include chants in the process of charging or burying.

5. Bury the Apple

You'll recall that candle magick primarily utilized the element of fire. Once the candle was charged with your intention, you lit the candle and let it burn away. Instead of burning the charged apple, you will bury it deep in the ground—this principally employs the element of earth rather than fire.

As the apple slowly and permanently decomposes from your reality, so will whatever you wish to banish. It will be absorbed back into the earth, and the energy dispersed away from your life.

Conclusion

Moon energy is just one kind of energy. It is potent and readily available any night of the year. Even during the new Moon, there is a kind of lunar energy to be had.

But lunar energy is not required to perform magic. You can perform spells that run counter to the Moon's energy if you call upon the Watchtowers, spirits, or even your ancestors. The Moon is powerful but it does not dictate everything.

And this is part of the balance that sits at the core of Wicca. In order to fully work with Moon magic, you must understand its benefits and limitations. Magic, like any other tool, is guided by both. And as you explore various branches of magic, you will find one that works best for you. This can only happen when you've taken the time to fully understand each branch you've explored. If Moon magic is where you find your magical home, embrace it. Bolster your spells with images of the Moon, songs in Her honor, and representations of all the Moon's phases. Call upon all aspects of the goddess and learn to walk in the shadows that fall when it is the dark of the Moon. You may also find that studying Moon magic leads you as much to astronomy as astrology. Do not fight this pull. Understanding the Moon and the celestial bodies that move around it will only serve to enhance your power. In your studies you will find that Moon magic intersects with other branches of celestial magic, such as star magic and Sun magic. Go where your studies leads you.

Learn and grow within the Moon's light. She is always ready to guide you

Wicca Book of Spells

How to perform your own Wiccan. Witches and Solitary Practitioners with Herbal Magic, Crystal Magic.
A Book to Cast Powerful Spells and Master Witchcraft.

Linda Candles

Introduction

W hen Wicca came out of the mist and went around the world, countless people began to identify with this religious manifestation and why it was the only one until that moment that had a female central deity as the creator. This was in the mid-1950s and extended into the 1970s and early 1970s, 80s.

From its inception in 1951, the Wicca has acquired new expectations and has undergone significant transformations, being hugged by the feminist and environmental movements, earning a new face which is much more matrifocal and Goddess-oriented than at the beginning of its history, relegating to God a secondary position.

It's understandable since the sacred male was revered for thousands of years, while the Goddess was mutilated and forgotten. It was in 1970 that the feminist movement embraced Wicca as their religion. "Official", finding in the Goddess a strong figure capable of causing changes deep in the thinking of society and its way of looking at the world. Many Feminist traditions emerged from this and contributed a substantial creative, quality material that would forever change Wicca!

Women who fought for gender equality rights found in this religion a safe haven to feel strong, alive, and active. It was in Wicca that they found a religion that can redeem their dignity, both social and religious. From the search for a new religion, a thought group where women were not were excluded rose in the US through the efforts of countless women engaged in feminist causes, a Wicca with a new identity more focused on the Goddess figure. From this growing movement came several traditions of this religion, from the branches where the Goddess and God are less visible and the Goddess exercises supremacy and preponderance.

Along with Wicca's growth and outreach in the mid-1980s, came the "rabeira" and several other Pagan movements. Druidism, Kemetism, Hellenism, Asatrú and other countless world Neopagan movements have only begun to be visible thanks to the efforts of Wiccans seeking to revive an Earth-centered religion, in the Sacred Feminine, in the search for connection with the flag of the struggle for freedom in strongly monotheistic countries, showing that each one can revere the Divine in his own way, rescuing almost forgotten rituals in the time. As Wicca brought in its structure Celtic, Nordic, Greek, Sumerians and whatever seemed correct, as these cultures connected with the heirs of the Goddess Religion over time, many groups separated, seeking for the spiritual and cultural identity of the Gods with which they felt more connected. Thus arose the reconstructionist movement, who try to reconstruct the worship of the ancient Gods exactly as it was in the past. Many people who had started belonging to these movements then began to criticize Wicca's flexibility, saying that she was not the true heiress of the European Religion, which was not Celtic, that Wicca was Gardner's invention, etc.

Even with contrary opinions, Wicca continued its climb and was experiencing a revolution within its own environment. Along with this, congresses, meetings, and seminars began to be held to discuss the practices of this religion in the US. Because of the many attacks on Wicca, one council, with the most renowned Wiccans of the time, was created to write the 13 Principles of Witchcraft, which was published in the form of public notice.

Wicca has been gaining strength and visibility worldwide as an official religion. In the United States and several other countries, officers of the beloved forces have the right to chaplaincy, which has been largely and unrestrictedly granted to Wiccan priests.

The first principle says, "Like American Witches, we don't feel threatened by debates about the history of art, the origins of various terms, the legitimacy of various aspects of different traditions. We are concerned about our present and our future. "

Along with this new identity that Wicca was beginning to assume, the Goddess as the center of worship of this religion was increasingly emphasized. She became invoked in the rites as "The Goddess of the Ten Thousand Names" (just like Isis, who was all Goddesses in one) and the statement that all Goddesses are the same Goddess is definitely accepted among the Wiccans and widely used in various segments of Paganism.

Wicca then becomes a religion that recognizes the Goddess as the Creator, the main deity and even though some Wiccans consider themselves polytheists (some consider themselves monotheistic, panentheistic or henotheistic), our religion reveres the one and only Goddess who manifests in different forms, names, and attributes.

If in the mid-1950s Wicca was considered much more a magical system rather than a religion, then today, the reality is completely different. Many Wiccan groups organized to legitimize it as a true religion, making it accepted, recognized and respected in different segments of society. Wicca's highest visibility is still in the United States and Europe where it is considered a chaplaincy religion in the army and marriages recognized by the State

In various countries, Wicca has been growing substantially. We see each day more and more literary works proposed to clarify its religious and philosophical aspects and we are constantly facing with people decorating our sacred symbols, like the Pentagram or the Triluna, in the subway, bus, bank queue or streets.

Today, there are a lot more people practicing the Art of Witchcraft alone than in groups, which are called Covens. She transformed from a secret religion into a modern alternative religiosity, strongly centered on the figure of the Goddess Mother and consciousness-oriented environmental and social groups of different ethnicities have incorporated much of their culture into Wicca, making it more flexible and therefore eclectic. The saying "All Goddesses are the Goddess" has become a Wiccan axiom since the last decade and so Hindu, Native American, African, Hawaiian, Chinese, and many other culture goddesses were assimilated by Wicca and came to be recognized as different faces of the Goddess.

Most of today's religions of mankind are based on figures and male divine principles, with Gods and Priests rather than Goddesses and Priestesses. For millennia, women's values have been put into many cultures in which women are subdued and occupy a lower position than men, whether at the social or spiritual level.

Wicca seeks to reclaim the Sacred Feminine and the role of women in religion, priestesses of the Great Mother, as well as the complementarity and balance between man and woman symbolized through the Goddess and God, who complement each other. Wicca gives the Goddess a leading role in both practices either in their myths, so it is the main deity worshiped and invoked in the sacred rites.

Chapter 1 Spells

For some spells, you will be asked to chant or say either a mantra or an incantation. These are words of your creation or that you have found elsewhere that very clearly state the intent of the magic you are attempting to perform & the outcome you are asking for. It is not necessary that you recite anything well-known or that is known by anyone else in the world, in fact. It is thought that there are certain words that you have to say in a certain order a certain number of times for magic to work. This is not true and is a misconception about witchcraft. Because the energy already exists out in the universe and you are merely asking for its assistance, it will respond to and recognize any words that you use as long as you are clear on what you're asking.

For oil being used in magic, you will need to also use a carrier oil, just like with every other type of essential oil. Certain oils are too strong to be used directly on the skin, therefore finding a carrier oil that works for you will make it safe to use.

Because everyone is allergic to different things, there are some ingredients and herbs that will cause allergic reactions in certain people. You must heed any advice from your doctor regarding things that you may be allergic to, such as nuts, oils, or Ragweed related herbs.

There are many different types of magic that we will use our Herbal Magic four.

They are each labeled based on the type of spell it is, some of which are multiple types of spells:

- Tea
- Milk
- Food
- Baths
- Sachet
- Oil
- Incense
- Charm

Specific Spells

Clear Bad Energy Charm

One of the first spells you will want to cast has to do with the space you are using. You will want to learn how to get rid of bad energy before doing magic there.

You will use dried Juniper to smudge the space by lighting it on fire and asking for the positive energy to send the negative energy out of the space. If you are indoors, you will want to leave a door or window open for the bad energy to leave.

Increase Good Energy Charm

Another great Basic Spell to have is encouraging positive energy in a space that you are about to do work in.

You will need Rosemary thyme and cinnamon, and for those dried herbs in a cup or bowl that can be used for incense or putting flame in two. You will light these herbs on fire and imagine the smoke emanating from it as providing the good energy for your space.

Bad Energy Person Sachet

Unfortunately, there are times when all of us will have to deal with people who are not our cup of magical tea. To protect yourself from their negative energy, you can make yourself a protective sachet.

Combine the Petals of Vervain and yarrow into a drawstring bag that can fit in your pocket while imagining a force field around the other person keeping all of their negativity into themselves and a warm white light emanating from the center of you out into the space around you. Carry this with you whenever you know you will be around them, or all the time to protect yourself from everyone's negative energy.

Full Moon Bath

If you are planning on doing any magic with the full moon or in the few days leading up to a Full Moon, it is helpful to take a full moon bath which will help to connect you with your magic.

In a warm bath combine half a cup of sea salt, a tablespoon of calendula flowers, a tablespoon of yarrow, a tablespoon of mugwort, and five drops of lavender oil. Rest in this bath for at least 15 minutes to cleanse your energy and prepare yourself for the power of Full Moon magic.

Money Charm or Incense

Of course, all of us would like a chance at acquiring more money, so use this simple spell to do so.

In an incense burner or Bowl, put a few basil leaves in the middle and use one or two drops of Patchouli oil on them. Light them on fire and chant a mantra asking to receive money.

Job Charm or Incense

If you are having work troubles, you can use this spell to help relieve them.

In an incense bowl or burner, you can use either the plants or herbs from frankincense or Sandalwood, or you can just use incense sticks or Cones just as well. Light it's on fire, blow it out, and let the smoke emanates as you chant a mantra about your job situation. Whether that be finding a new job, finding Harmony in your current job, or changing an aspect of your career, ask the universal energy for assistance and you shall receive it.

Love Tea and Oil

If you are looking to find love, this tea will assist you. However, it also requires the use of oil on your skin in addition to ingesting the tea.

You will need a tea from a flowering plant or tree, such as hibiscus, cherry, or Apple. Most likely these will be caffeine-free herbal teas. You can purchase them pre-made or make them yourself. You should put a single drop of Jasmine oil into a carrier oil before applying it to your pressure points, such as your wrists behind your ears and on the back of your knee caps. Then drink the tea you have made and chant a mantra about accepting love into your life.

Health Incense or Oil

To promote a general sense of well-being and stay in good health, you can use this simple Vitality incense of burning either eucalyptus incense or heating eucalyptus oil on a candle warmer.

Lasting Love Charm and Food

If you already have a person that you love and you would like to keep your love everlasting, you can take an apple, split it in two, each of you eat 1/2, and bury the seeds or core in your yard. This will make sure that your love continues to grow.

Lost Objects Sachet

If you have lost or forgotten something, an easy way to cast a spell is to put a couple of almonds into a sachet with the intention of finding your way.

Night Protection Charm

A great way to protect your energy while you sleep is to put something Pine above your bed. This can be a branch, a bundle of pine needles, or you could even have a pine headboard.

Hunting Protection Charm

If you have the feeling that there is some sort of negative energy haunting your space, you can put lilacs in and around that area to keep them away from you.

Sun Positivity Charm

If you are looking for a pick-me-up or a bit of sunshine on a gloomy day, placing an orange, orange rind, or part of an orange tree on your windowsill will harness the energy of the Sun and bring it into your house. This will bring you healing properties, energy, and a sense of Happiness.

Parasite Incense or Oil

This can be either literally or emotionally if there is some sort of bug that is eating away at either your plants or your energy, any herb in the mint family will resolve this. For physical manifestations, you will want to sprinkle peppermint oil on the ground in the area. For mental irritations, you will want to burn peppermint incense.

Breaking a Curse Charm

If you have reason to believe that a curse has been put on you, you will want to use chili pepper, even red pepper flakes from the pizza parlor, to protect yourself. Spread the pepper around the base of your bed before you go to sleep, and in the morning sweep it up and throw it away outside. You can do this for as many nights in a row as you think is necessary.

Blessing Charm

Similarly, to ask for and receive blessings, you can spread the flowers of the chamomile plant around the base of your bed before you go to sleep. In the morning sweep them up and throw them away outside. You can do this for as many nights in a row as you think is necessary.

Courage Food

If you have an event coming up in which you know you will need the courage to get through it, you can sprinkle a bit of dried thyme on your food and eat it. This can be eaten alone or with other food.

Friendship Incense and Food

If you are looking for someone to whom you can rely upon and become good and true friends, you can use clove to do so. This can be used in food, such as is common to glaze a ham with, or you can merely burn incense to draw this positive friendship to you.

Communicating Across Planes Tea or Sachet

If you are planning to communicate with someone or something in a different plane of existence, dandelions are especially helpful for this purpose. You can make a tea from it; they also sell it to pre-made. Or you could put a few dandelions into a drawstring back to carry with you.

Passion Tea and Food

If you have a lover that you would like to infuse some passion into, both of you can use ginger for these purposes. You can make a tea of it or use it in your food.

Attracting men sachet

If you are looking to attract a man, you can use Orris root to do so. Used most effectively as a powder, it often smells like violets. For this reason, you can place some Orris root in any form into a sachet along with rose in any form, most especially its pedals. Carrying this around with you will attract male attention from all passersby.

Protecting Others Sashay

If you are wanting to form a protective barrier for another person, you can use Angelica root in a sachet to give them to carry around. It is most effective if you also combine it with part of a birch tree, whether that is its bark, leaf, or some of its wood.

Ritualistic Charm

If you want to convey the importance and consecrate any tool you're using, spell you're performing, magic you are using or face you are using, you can use B hyssop herb to smudge to purify, cleanse, and elevate.

Nightmare Protection Cachet

Some people are plagued with nightmares, and to protect them from the negative energy in their dreams, you can make them a sachet that they will place under their pillow at night. In it, you can use rosemary, dill, and Heather to protect them while they are in the unconscious plane of existence.

Controlling Your Dreams Sachet

If you have the feeling that someone is trying to communicate with you within your dreams, you can increase your ability to experience this by using nutmeg and bay leaves in a sachet that you place under your pillow at night. This increases your luck and chance of having an encounter in this spiritual plane.

Creative Boost Sachet

If you are looking for an increase in your creativity, you can place Hawthorne sprigs or any part of the Hawthorn tree in your workspace to give yourself a boost.

Increase Your Business Charm

If you are a business owner, you can increase the number of customers you have and the amount of money you make by play Sing part of the Pennyroyal herb over the door the customer's walkthrough. It is important to remember that Pennyroyal should not be handled by anyone who is or could be pregnant.

Magical Thinking Incense

If you are working on your spiritual journey and you want to communicate across planes and acquire wisdom, you can burn Sage to purify the space before you begin as well as it assisting in your journey to the other side.

Banishing Charm

If you feel that something negative or evil energy is attached to you, you can use every day black pepper and order to break this curse. If you were someone you know would like to be rid of this energy, simply spread black pepper and a circle around you or that person while chanting a mantra about exercising the evil from the person and the space.

Diet Charm and Food

If you are having issues surrounding what you can and cannot eat and the emotional attachment that you have to certain types of food, you can use fennel to help alleviate this. You can use fennel in the food you are eating, or you can sprinkle fennel around your kitchen while chanting the mantra about alleviating your food is shoes.

Energy Stealing Charm and Food

Not only does garlic protect against traditionally fabled vampires, but it also helps to protect against people who drain your energy and Life Source. So, garlic can be used by you to either consume in food or bye sprinkling in a circle around you while chanting a mantra about protecting your energy.

Heal a Broken Heart Food

If you are feeling especially sad and broken-hearted, using marjoram in your food will help to ease the pain.

Grounding Charm

If you are about to begin any type of Magic Ritual or if you simply feel like you are out of touch with Mother Earth, you can use onion powder below your feet if you are standing, or below your bottom, if you are sitting on the ground. This will help to provide a conduit to allow you to become more physically and spiritually grounded before you perform magic.

Festival Preparation Charm

If you are looking to prepare your home to most effectively celebrating the upcoming holiday or Festival, you can use a branch or twig of the Rowan tree to protect your space. Walk around the space shaking the branch and chanting a mantra about protection. When you are finished, hang that branch above the door and it will last until the next Festival.

Good Memory Charm

If you are in a relationship and you are watching to remember or encourage positive and good memories that you have there, you can use Periwinkle for this. Taking a Periwinkle flower, you will hold it in your hands and chant a spell of your creation to draw forth positive memories you have with another person. When you have finished your incantation, place the flower in a book to be pressed and preserved.

Remembering Those Who Have Passed Incense

If you are honoring or remembering someone who has died, a very common way to do so is to light incense of acacia. You can use any part of this tree, the leaves, or twigs. It is understood that this bush and tree are associated with both Judaism and Christianity, making it an especially powerful spell.

Communicating with Those Who Have Passed Charm

If you are having a séance or communication of any kind with people in different Realms, you can use African Blackwood to increase your communication Pathways and two protect yourself when reaching into the other realm. By simply holding on to a twig or a black of this type of wood, you will use it as a channel.

Healing Spaces After Emergencies Charm

If there was an emergency or a traumatic event in a space, whether that be a natural catastrophe or a man-made tragedy, you can use the wood of the ailanthus tree to help heal that space. If you build a fire using this wood, you can chant an incantation to send the world's healing to that environment.

Resurrection Charm

This is not recommended for any witch who is new to the religion, but it is one of the most well-known spells in witchcraft. If one were to attempt to resurrect someone or something back to life, the use of Alder Wood, especially in the form of a magic wand, is the best way to do so. However, because it is very powerful and also can be unpredictable, this is not recommended.

Stress Tea

If you are looking for a quick fix for an overabundance of stress in your life, you can create a tea using chamomile, hops, and valerian root. This will help create calm in your life. If you would like, you can also add one drop of lavender.

To Divine Tea

If you are looking to prepare yourself for an especially rigorous magic spell in which you look into other planes of existence, you can make a tea using any kind of caffeinated leaf, mugwort, any part of a rose, and lemon balm. This will help give you the energy, focus, and spiritual guidance to cross the planes.

Protection Tea

If you are looking to be protected either physically or spiritually, you can use any type of caffeinated tea, valerian root, hyssop, and comfrey to give you a level of protection.

Grounding Tea

If you are looking for a way to become more grounded and your life or magic, you can create this comment and tasty tea. Using any type of caffeinated Tea Leaf, hibiscus, hyssop, chamomile, hops, Rose, and linden, you will be using so many elements of the mother earth that it will assist you in becoming one with her.

To Purify Tea

If you feel like you need to be purified before a ritual or if you have something attached to you, you can create a tea to cleanse yourself. Using any type of caffeinated tea, chamomile, valerian root, hyssop, and fennel, will help cleanse your spirit.

Clairvoyant Tea

If you are trying to communicate across different planes of existence, you can use this tea to do so. Use a mint-based tea, adding rosemary, thyme, and mugwort. This will assist in your ability to reach across the other worlds.

Cold and Flu Relief Tea

To heal yourself from either a cold or the flu, you can create an herbal tea that does not contain caffeine by combining chamomile, Ginger, valerian root, dandelion, lemon balm oh, and mint. This will rejuvenate your senses and provide healing and calmness to you.

Fever Tea

If you are trying to relieve yourself of a fever, you can create an herbal, caffeine-free tea using cinnamon, marjoram, Thyme, and ginger.

Muscle Pain Tea

If you are looking to relieve muscle pains or cramps, you can create a caffeine-free tea using chamomile, valerian root, and ginger.

Settle the Stomach Tea

If you are looking for a way to settle an upset stomach, you can create this caffeine-free tea using mint leaves, Ginger, chamomile, and marjoram.

Coughing Tea

If you are looking to relieve a cough, you can create a tea using mint leaves, yarrow, and One Singular drop of cinnamon spoil.

Natural Energy Tea

If you are looking for a natural energizing Tea without caffeine, you can make it using orange peels, ginger, cinnamon, lemon balm, and coriander.

Good Dreams Tea

If you are looking to sleep well and encourage good dreams, you can make a tea out of mint leaves, hibiscus, chamomile, and Valerian root.

Digestion Tea

If you are looking for a simple and effective way to improve your digestion after eating, you can make a very basic T using only fennel seeds. This is simple but classic.

Sensual Tea

If you are looking for a romantic tea to sip with a partner, you can make this tea. Using mint leaves, rose petals or rosehip oil, orange peel, and cinnamon, you will have a very passionate and lovely caffeine-free tea.

Sadness Tea

If you are looking to overcome a sense of sadness, you can make this caffeine-free tea to help you cheer up. Take nettle leaves, St John's Wort, mint leaves, and cinnamon. These will help your spirit and energy.

Evening Relaxation Tea

If you would simply like to have a lovely evening routine, you can create this tea to Aid in your ritual. Use mint leaves, chamomile, lemon verbena, a drop of lavender, and a drop of rosehip oil. When did together, this will be reminiscent of taking a walk through a fresh French garden at Sunset.

Insomnia Tea

If you are having difficulty sleeping, you can create this caffeine-free herbal tea for just such occasions. Combine mint leaves, chamomile, and Vervain root or leaves to lull yourself back to sleep.

Migraine Tea

If you suffer from migraines, a good natural solution would be to make this type of tea for yourself. Combine valerian root, the flowers of a linden tree, or the berries of a linden tree, berries of a juniper tree, and St. John's Wort.

Anxiety Tea

If you suffer from anxiety, a good way to settle your nerves is by creating this type of tea. Combine chamomile, hops, St John's Wort, a drop of Jasmine oil, and a drop of lavender.

Nausea Tea

If you are feeling nauseous or sick to your stomach, you can create this tea to settle it. Use chamomile, clove, and Ginger.

Stomach in Knots Tea

If you are nervous about something and your tummy is tied, you can create this tea to calm yourself. Use lemon balm, Angelica, and fennel seeds, as well as lemon and lemon Pele, if you wish.

Happiness Bath

If you are feeling the need to invite more happiness into your life, you can add these things to your bath: Rose petals, jasmine flowers, Epsom salt, lavender flowers, orange peels. If you do not have the actual flowers of any of these things, you can substitute them out for other types of flowers or the oils of those things. Chant a happiness incantation as you immerse yourself in the water.

Aching Muscles Bath

If you are overworked or you are simply feeling pain around your body, you can create a healing and magical bath for yourself. Add Epsom salt, Sage, lavender, eucalyptus, and mint to the water to soothe your body. You can use the leaves or flowers of any of these in addition to their oils.

Improve Circulation Bath

To improve the blood circulation within your body, you can take a warm bath and add nettle, marigold flowers, and ginger. You can use the root or the powder of any of these, as well.

Skin Relief Bath

If your skin is feeling irritated or inflamed, you can take a bath and order to relieve this discomfort. Add any part of an alder tree, dandelion, and meant to the water.

Love Bath

If you are looking to attract more love and romance into your life, you can take a beautiful bath by adding lavender, Rosemary, mint, and time to your bath.

Renewal Bath

If you would like to refresh and renew your energy concerning anything, in particular, you can use this very effective bath. Add rose petals, cinnamon, and Eucalyptus to the water to renew the energy around you.

Career Bath

If you are looking to change your career, get clarification within a job, or find a new job, you can take this bath. Add rosemary leaves and cinnamon while you chant a mantra asking for guidance in your career.

Green Magic Bath

If you are looking to increase your connection and build trust with any type of deity or Mother Earth who celebrates the soil and grounding, you can create this bath for yourself. Use lavender, Rosemary, mint leaves, rose petals, lemon balm, orange peels, lavender oil, Patchouli oil, and rose oil to create unofficially Bounty around you in the water.

Sleeplessness Milk

If you are looking for a way to prevent sleeplessness at night you can create this magic Moon milk to help you. Using any type of milk that you prefer, add cinnamon, turmeric, cardamom, ginger, nutmeg, and black pepper to prepare your body to sleep soon.

Sweet Dreams Milk

If you want to attract sweet and loving dreams to yourself tonight, you can create this Milk. Using any type of milk, you'd like, add lavender petals, and vanilla.

Warmth milk

If you are looking to simply get warmer and be cozy for the night, you can make this tea. Use any type of milk you prefer, add Ginger, cinnamon oh, and cardamom.

Spring Sleep Milk

If you are looking for a Fresh & Light way to end your evening, you can create this milk. Using dried chamomile flowers and vanilla, this is a delightful bedtime treat.

Love Milk

If you want to spend your evening attracting love to yourself, you can drink this love milk before bed. Using hibiscus, vanilla, rose, cinnamon, and Nutmeg along with your milk of choice, this will help attract romance into your life.

Purity Oil

If you are looking for an oil for rituals to purify a tool, you can create it by adding Juniper oil, Cedar wood oil, and lavender.

Consecrate Oil

If you want to begin a ritual with the most magical power possible you can use this oil for your tools, alter, or space. Add cinnamon, myrrh, and frankincense.

Blessing Oil

If you are performing a ritual and which you ask for a blessing or if you are merely working a spell for yourself, you can use this on any tools, Babs, or spaces. Combined patchouli, Orange oh, and Sandalwood.

Protection Oil

If you are feeling negative energy in your space, you can use this around yourself, space, or another person. Patchouli, mugwort, lavender, birch, and hyssop.

Grateful Oil

If you are wanting to show thanks for your appreciation to someone or something in any plane, you can create this oil for that ritual. Combine Rose, cinnamon, and clover.

Income Oil

If you are looking for a way to bring more funds into your life, you can use this concoction to do so. Combine orange, ginger, sandalwood, and patchouli to create this attracting money or funds.

Easy Breathing Oil

If you are congested or having difficulty breathing, you can combine these oils to create a spell. Add mint, eucalyptus, and benzoin too hot water and inhale the steaming Magic.

Lust Oil

If you are looking for a way to instigate lust towards yourself in another person, you can use the soil for those bells. Combine Caraway, vanilla, cinnamon, Rose, and Ginger.

Passion Oil

If you are looking to create passion in a relationship that you already have, you can't use this oil in a spell. Combined cardamom, chili pepper, Ginseng, and Jasmine.

Joint Oil

If you are having joint pain or issues, then this will help you find relief. Combine chamomile, mint, and comfrey. This can be applied topically for a spell.

Relationship Oil

If you are looking to improve the relationship that you have with another person, you can create the soil to assist. Combined coriander, Beechwood, cherry, and rosehip oil to be used in a spell.

Harmony Oil

If you are looking to communicate across different planes, you are going to want to make sure that everything is in Harmony in order not to bring any negative energy back with you. For these rituals, you can create and oil mixing in Cypress, Elder, eucalyptus, myrrh, and frankincense.

Attraction Oil

If you are looking to attract a partner, you can increase your appeal by using this oil in a spell. Combine Dragon's blood, lemon verbena, and Juniper.

Underworld Oil

If you are looking to do some work with the afterlife and other planes of existence, specifically communicating with the dead, you will want to create an oil to increase your Effectiveness and protection. Combine parsley, patchouli, Cedar, and Fir oils for these rituals and spells.

Open heart Incense

If you are wanting to make yourself more open and welcoming to the world into love, you can create this incense to do so. Combine Juniper, dragon's blood, dried leaves of an orange tree, myrrh, rose petals, and Sassafras.

Happy home Incense

If you want to create a safe and happy place for yourself and others to call home, you can create this incense to do so. Combine Sage, dried leaves from the linden tree, honeysuckle, and ivy.

Pure house Incense

If you would like to clear a house or space of any negative energy that you think might have been attracted or attached to it, you can create this incense for that purpose. Combined myrrh, frankincense, dragon's blood, Dill, rose petals, and Sandalwood.

Exorcism Incense

If, however, you have a more intense attachment of negative energy that has to be fully exercise, you can use this incense to do so. Combine bay leaves, mugwort, frankincense, St John's Wort, Angelica, Rosemary, and Basil.

Refreshing Incense

If you are looking to fill a space with a sense of renewal and refreshments, you can create this incense to set that mode. Combined Sandalwood, lemon verbena, Vervain, cinnamon, and bay leaves.

Banish Negativity Incense

If you feel like there is a negative energy in an area, you can use this incense to cleanse the space. Combined bay leaves, cloves, marjoram, oregano, and Time.

End Attachments Incense

If you would like to close off an attachment that is connected to a person or a thing or a space, you can use this incense for those smudging purposes. Combine cinnamon, myrrh, bay leaves, and rose petals.

Lasting Love Incense

If you would like to have an everlasting love with your partner, you can create this incense to burn at night. Combine vanilla, Wintergreen, peppermint, and Jasmine.

Blessing Incense

If you are looking to bless a space for personal reasons or before a ritual, you can use this incense for that purpose. Combine lavender, hyssop, basil, and the leaves from a flowering plant, such as orange leaves, lemon leaves, Apple leaves, or cherry leaves.

Hex Removal Incense

If you believe that a hex has been put upon someone or something, you can use this incense to undo the hex. Combined clove, frankincense, fur, and Holly.

Peace Incense

If you would like to promote a sense of peace and Harmony in a space, you can create this innocence to do so. Combine lavender, lemon, Orris root, and cardamom.

Spiritual Protection Incense

If you are looking for protection when communicating across different planes, you can use this incense to do so. Combine myrrh, cinnamon, bay leaves, and cloves.

Anti Thievery Incense

If you have recently had something stolen or if you think something might have been stolen or if you want to prevent something from being stolen, you can use this incense to cast the spell around it. Combine Ivy, Rosemary, Honeysuckle, and Juniper and use it in a spell.

Psychic Protection Incense

If you feel like someone is manipulating you mentally or emotionally or spiritually, you can use this incense for Extra Protection. Combine Elder Leaf, bay leaves, Valerian, basil, dragon's blood, frankincense, patchouli, and Sandalwood.

Growing Love Incense

If you have a budding relationship that you would like to see grow stronger, whether that is romantic or in Friendship, you can use this incense to help move your relationship along. Combine basil, Bergamot, Rose, lavender, and Sandalwood.

Attract Men Incense

If you are specifically looking to attract men to you romantically, you can use this incense to encourage those attractions. Combine Pine, Sandalwood, Orris root, myrrh, frankincense, Patchouli, and Jasmine.

Harmony Incense

If you have a relationship that needs help Becoming Harmonious, you can use this in a sentence to correct your partnership. Combine myrrh, cinnamon, cardamom, ginger, and coriander.

Go Away Incense

If you have someone or something that you wish would leave you alone and stop giving you attention, you can use this incense to distract and dissuade them. Combine mistletoe, Sage, Orris root, and bay leaves.

Break up Incense

If you are looking to break up with someone else, or if someone else has broken up with you and you would like to get over the pain, you can use this instance to help with that growth. Combined balm of Gilead, Patchouli, lemongrass, and Dogwood.

Fertility Incense

If you are looking for assistance in the process of conception, you can use this incense to assist the process. Combine mistletoe, St John's Wort, Mandrake, and Cherry.

Friends Forever Incense

If you are looking to make sure that you and your friend keep a close and healthy relationship for all of your life, you can use this incense to help with a spell. Combine Rosemary, Elder, frankincense, Dogwood, and yarrow.

Ending Incense

If you are looking to help something come to a close or an end, you can use this incense to encourage that Journey. Combined lemon balm, Bay, Willow, peppermint, gyro, and Penny Royal.

Virility Incense

If you are a man who is looking to become more feral, you can use this incense to increase your stamina. Combine Holly, Mandrake, dragon's blood, Oak, and patchouli.

Good Business Incense

If you are looking to encourage your business ventures on a prosperous Journey, use this incense in the place of business. Combined benzoin, basil, and cinnamon.

Money Incense

If you are looking to find an increase in the flow of money into your life, you can use this incense. Combine frankincense, nutmeg, cinnamon, and lemon balm.

Confidence Incense

If you are looking for a boost of self-confidence, use this incense to increase it. Combine garlic, chamomile, Rosemary, and Cedar.

Determined Incense

If you are looking for help staying the course and being determined, you can use this incense to increase it. Combine chamomile, time, St John's Wort, Oak, and Willow.

Luck Incense

If you have been playing the lottery or are simply looking to find a little good luck in your life, you can use this incense to increase your chances. Combine dragon's blood, Linden, mistletoe, Rose, and clover.

Success Incense

If you have something in your life that you are hoping we'll be successful, you can use this incense to encourage it. Combine mistletoe, sunflower, onion, sandalwood, cedar, and myrrh.

Wisdom Incense

If you are looking for another level of wisdom to come into your spirit, you can use this incense on that Journey. Combine Angelica, Vervain, clove, bay leaves, benzoin, and Sage.

Legal Incense

If you have a legal concern or a situation with the law, you can use this incense to help make sure it goes in your favor. Combine Sandalwood, onion, cascara, St John's wort, and Oak.

Basic Healing Incense

If you would like a simple healing incense that can be used for anyone at any time, this is a great combination. Use both Rosemary and Juniper.

Sickness Incense

If you are already sick and are looking to help heal yourself, you can use this incense to overcome a cold or the flu. Come by and cloves, Juniper, eucalyptus, Wintergreen, and Willow.

Congestion Incense

If you are having difficulty breathing due to congestion or restricted airways, you can use this incense to help. Come by and pine, Cedar, eucalyptus, and mint.

Beauty Incense

If you are looking to increase how beautiful you appear to others, you can combine these to create and encourage your beauty. Combined Angelica, cherry, Linden, Rose, and Elder.

Hope Incense

If you are looking to come out of a funk and find New Hope in the world, you can use this incense to help you. Combine time, cloves, chamomile, Patchouli, and Willow.

Chapter 2 Consecrating Your Tools

Whether you choose to practice magick exclusively in sacred space or to incorporate your magickal practice into your everyday life, it is often necessary and appropriate to dedicate certain tools solely for ritual use. When this happens, a consecration ritual is needed to lend your items their proper intention for magickal use.

Consecrating your tools and reserving them for ritual use will keep their energies clear and focused, which lends even more power to their effectiveness in spell work and manifestation. Furthermore, consecrating your tools deepens your religious devotion to the craft and shows the elements and gods that you are serious about your practice and are willing to show yourself and them the respect and reverence that are appropriate to a true practitioner of Wicca.

Choosing Deities for Your Ritual

Choosing deities for your consecration rituals is no small task. Some may choose to invoke the same deities that one is dedicated to for all consecration rituals. Others may choose different gods and goddesses for each tool, based on the specific use and intention behind each one. For example, Cerridwen might preside over a consecration ritual for a cauldron due to her association with cauldrons, while another goddess might be invoked for consecrating the chalice, athame, and wand.

It is important to exercise caution and respect when invoking deities for any kind of ritual. It is generally regarded as poor form to invoke deities from different pantheons within the same ritual, and it is common sense to never invoke warring deities to consecrate your ritual tools, lest your items always be at war with one another.

If gods from different pantheons are chosen for different items, it would be best to hold different consecration rituals for each tool to prevent mixing deities. If all tools are consecrated to the same deities, however, then only one ritual may be necessary—unless, of course, your guidance moves you to hold multiple rituals at different times, or if you acquire a new item after the others. Use your best judgment when choosing the deities, you wish to invoke in your consecration rituals, and do plenty of research to know the best energies for each tool and the most appropriate pairings of deities in your rituals.

Invoking the Elements

Just as in any ritual, it is important to ask all the elements to be present during your consecration ritual. The elements will work with and through every tool regardless of its uses or associations, so it is crucial that they are all present at the consecration ceremony to familiarize themselves with your intended tools.

That being said, some tools will fall more completely under the domain of one element over the others depending on their uses and intentions. For example, athames and swords are associated primarily with the air element, while chalices are associated with water, censers with fire, and mortar and pestle with earth. If you choose to consecrate one item per ritual, it is appropriate to have the tool's predominant element present in a bigger way within the ritual to help channel and boost its energy into the item itself.

Casting a Circle

Casting a circle is the traditional method of setting sacred space in the Wiccan tradition. Circle casting forms the backbone of every Wiccan ritual, creating continuity and consistency throughout every spell and ritual in one's magickal practice.

Before casting a circle, it is important that one get grounded and centered to sharpen concentration and focus one's personal energy. Before working with other energies, one must first learn to control one's own energy, keeping it calm and grounded at all times during a ritual.

A good grounding and centering meditation are as follows: in either a sitting or standing position, take a few deep breaths to relax the body and clear the mind, bringing your focus to your breath itself. After a few moments of breathing in silence, bring your attention to your heart center, pressing your palms together over your chest with your elbows out. Feel the strength in your upper body as you gently press your palms together and feel the box formed by your elbows and shoulders. Next, move your attention down to your hips and legs. Feel the strength in your legs and feet, knowing that they always support you perfectly. Then, move your attention down to the ground, allowing a growing awareness of the earth beneath you. Feel how the earth always supports you, and soak in the strength and stability that this brings. As this awareness grows, envision roots growing from the bottoms of your feet down into the earth. These roots slowly stretch down, down, down into the center of the Earth, passing underground springs and hidden stores of crystals, deep down into the Earth's magma core. As you access the molten and rocky core of the Earth, slowly begin to draw the energy up through your roots. Envision the red energy coming up from the molten lava deep within the Earth, moving up past the crystal stores and the underground streams, up into your feet, filling your body one inch at a time. Move the energy up through your legs, your hips, your torso, your shoulders, your arms, your neck, and your head. Take a few deep breaths as this energy fills you completely, then slowly return the energy back down to the earth, breathing slowly as it moves back down to your feet. Feel the solid ground beneath you. Feel the strength in your legs and feet. When you feel completely grounded and centered, open your eyes and proceed with casting the circle.

The circle can be cast using visualization, smudging, tools like wands and athames, drumming, crystals, feathers, or your hands. The athame is the most traditional tool used for circle casting with its ability to symbolically "cut" the energy separating the mundane world from the spiritual one.

Some Wiccans begin drawing their circles in the east, in correlation with the rising sun and the springtime, while others start at the north, in correlation with the top of the compass and the north's association with the earth element, which helps to ground the energy of the circle. Choose the method that works best for you, either through consulting your specific tradition or experimenting with different methods. Next, you'll need to draw energy down into you so that you can channel it into the casting of the circle. After you have cleared your own energy and kept it grounded and centered, raise your arms over your head. If you are using a tool, hold it in your dominant hand, which is associated with projecting energy rather than receiving it.

Draw the energy from the divine universal source down through your crown and feel it charging up towards your hands and tool. As the energy builds, slowly focus it through the tips of your fingers or your tool, slowly releasing it as you walk or turn to create your circle in a clockwise, or deosil, direction.

Chapter 3 Money Magic Spells

How to Attract Money and Manifest Abundance

Money is not the yardstick to experience things; most people consider money, character or behavior, and freedom to be similar thing. And it is important for awareness of our right to freedom, which is tantamount to our relationship with money, as this is one of the central themes in life experience. Hence, it is not a new thing or discovery that we have such a strong feeling for money.

They are many patterns of thought about making money, how you feel about the idea, and the amount of money you want to flow into your account. If you can put these thoughts into an aligned consciousness, you will exploit the powers of the world, and the sky's your limit in terms of your financial success. The most important thing in any financial situation is to categorically understand where the struggles stem from. White magic can give your business a new look, which will help you attract more money and shoot you to greater success.

Money Magic

The Right Way of Thinking

Lack of money makes you fear and feel discomforted when you think or speak about it, but the reverse is the case when you feel joy and well-being and think about the prosperity and comfort you will get from it. The dissimilarity is substantial, the reason being that the second statement creates money and the first takes money away from you.

How your mind thinks about money is very important and significant, and more outstanding is your feeling for money. "This is beautiful, how can I afford it?" Thoughts like this portray the sign that can siphon our attitude to wealth and prosperity. Therefore, it is paramount to understand what is not right with our thoughts and attitudes. If you can fathom your problems then will you able to change and fix them. Instead of dissatisfaction or lack, which is impossible to meet at the moment, your focus should be basically on what you need. Not its absence. Framing your mind in right direction is paramount to your success.

Many associates frequently with the feeling of lack having sufficient in their lives. Simply because they lack the ability to think far beyond the experience. Instead, if money is in limited supply and they have the knowledge of it and speak of it without taking maximum measure to maintain its stability. Extend yourself and leave your identity so that you can achieve your desire. Improve yourself on a daily basis to meet your goals and be successful. Our manner of thinking creates our life; the way we think manifests our reality. Transform your philosophy and be thankful for everything; then you will attract additional experience well-intentioned of being thankful. Such transformation is magical.

The Most Important Thing Is to Find a Balance

You need to be balanced inside out, do not just rely or depend on your inner harmony; strengthen but also explore what you accumulate in your thoughts or mind. Stay focused on your state of well-being, your actions. Your health also matters a lot.

From most people's perspective this will arise from an atmosphere of lack, which really is not the case. In many circumstances people may demand or need something purposely because they lack it, and as soon as they possess it, they are yet not satisfied, the inside reason being that there is constant thing that they lack. As a result of that it becomes an infinite struggle for them due to imbalance.

In the terms of the sacred, Tyr symbolizes success and victory in hunt in the Norse god Tiw's rune. The mighty warrior and honorable ally in times of necessity. Tyr is the first of eight in the runic alphabet according to traditional rules. So, all of the strength, blessings, perseverance and determination of this Deity can aid you. Whenever you demand the magical possessions of this rune, they will reinforce your determination together with your imagination, in such a way that your quest for business booming or for your well-paying employment will be compensated with achievement. It may be of interest in this illustration that Tyr reminds you of an arrow. This symbolizes how significant it is to devise a flawless goal in thoughts when looking for job. The rune similarly features refuge, which recommends this very spell is for the needy and should not be utilized by the greedy. Thus, real success remains possible. Just put in more effort and dedication and it will be within your grip in a short period of time.

To Turn on the Charm

Time: To achieve your goals sort out this spell in the course of a crescent moon. Wednesday is the preeminent day as it marks the time and day of understanding and the planet Mercury. Another important day is Tuesday, this is so called after the god Tiw and is taken by a lot as the second-best choice.

Spell Application

1. Create a circle as directed

2. Light up a candle with the following words of command. "Spirit of success secure me, look over me, and hold me."

3. Hold a piece of flint firmly in your palms, and envision yourself happy and also contented on your way to your place of work with a bag filled with money.

4. When prepared, take a very deep breath in then breathe on top of the stone as you assume the entirety of what you just requested will be conveyed onto the stone. And say, "By my breath I command strength to you."

5. Paint the Tyr on the flat part of the stone; allow it to lie out and dry next to the candle.

6. The following day, put the stone into your coat or trouser pocket and move with it at all times. When your request comes to pass, jettison the stone in the nearest source of natural water.

What You Will Need

A 15–20 cm yellow candle high during the time when you want to perform the spell on Wednesday or 15–20 cm red candle high if you wish to perform the spell on Tuesday. A lighter or box of matches is important for lighting your candle. A small stone that has a flat surface; it should be small and light enough to be worn in your trouser or jacket pocket.

More on Success Magic and Money Magic

Sometimes you may feel like the whole thing is occurring for some particular reason. Those particular people are destined to be luckier while others always seem to have bad luck. Such measures are not mere coincidence. Knowingly or not, events are the outcome of the precise, accurate plans and collaborations of others. We can assist you in achieving your dreams and goals, so that you can be among those who have more luck, by helping you make your dreams and goals come true.

- Voodoo ritual
- The work lamp
- Money magic rituals
- Success magic, money magic - white magic

What You Will Need

- One coconut
- One candle wick
- Heart meat (you can get this at your local supermarket)
- Red wine
- Oil
- Bones

Get two small wood pieces or coconut and tie them together as a support for the candlewick.

It is very important that you create this lamp for subsequent ease of access or a link to the lamp. Cut the coconut in half first, then bring three stones (put them under the coconut) to as its support, preventing it from tipping over. To maintain safety, it is recommended that you place the coconut on the center of a cooking tray, alternatively you can utilize another tray or pan that has high sides should the oil leak. Never remove the coconut pulp because it prevents oil from dripping out. If the pulp is removed the coconut will obviously leak boiling oil, which can be dangerous.

Next, take the bone then push it into the heart meat, as if you were pushing a single finger inside clay.

Place the heart meat, together with bone, inside the coconut then pour seven drops of red wine on top. While the red wine is dripping, voice out your wishes then call Legba.

Next, pour hot oil onto the bone with the heart meat; be careful not to fill the coconut past halfway. While pouring this oil, focus on the lamp and Legba.

Now carry two sticks, coconut or bamboo, and lay them over one another in an X shape. You may like to attach them to one another with candlewick or string.

Afterward, place your candlewick amidst your two pieces of bamboo. And very carefully hold the top edge of the candlewick and place it into the oil. Note that the bamboo should be floating on top of the oil and leave the wick top out of the oil. Then submerge the bottom of the wick.

Make sure the lamp is kept burning till you obtain the desired result.

Being mindful of Legba is one of the strongest Loa, and it not should not be called upon unnecessarily because this could cause very serious consequences.

Steps to Be Taken Towards Success and Money

Verifiable stats inform us that lack of money and financial problems are the major key reasons for divorce and end many relationships generally. Experience also contributes much and enlightens us to the fact that many with a good standard living are in a position to find a partner much easier compared to those suffering financial difficulties. Below are some clues that can help you mend your financial issues:

1. Develop a positive attitude towards money. Many dares and for some time try their best to be nice but think unconsciously that money is not clean. They also hold the distorted notion that when someone is rich, the person must be vicious. If these ideas also exist in your mind or thinking, will are unlikely to become rich. It is obvious that money is typically the energy. Money is not negative or positive like people's activities. You need to alter your thinking towards money if you want to earn more money (you can try to use tools like meditation or hypnosis). You can say and, experience it within, "I am attracting the abundance of money. This energy of abundance is good and I like to attract good things."

2. Establish a prosperity strategy on knowledge. It is no longer news nowadays that it is hardly possible to earn a lot of money by doing simple jobs and manual activities. Anything that can be automatized will be automatized and many jobs are done by automatic machines and robots. Soon simple jobs like booking clerk or taxi driver will vanish. The way to make more money is by being different or unique through knowing things others don't know, like an expert in a particular area. Invest money in your personal education.

3. Define your path or direction and goal. It is important to invest your time in learning some foreign languages; learn about whatever you find attractive; you can learn psychology, design or mechanical engineering. By learning, you are exposed to different people and new, inspiring ideas that will likely broaden your perspective. This can get you wonderful business ideas and approaches too. Your big money drive will be easier when you do what you like and enjoy. Your way of doing should be different and always do what gives you meaning.

Unfortunately, many don't know what they want simply because they don't have a clear and defined goal. Assuming you have in your account 300000000 dollars, what is the first thing you will do? Many people's idea would be: "If I had such money, I would take some time to tour different countries," or, "I would throw a big surprise party."

Another scenario is imagining that you died. What legacy would you like to give to the world? What message would be worth remembering about the life you lived? The most important thing is to start somewhere despite lack of money or time.

4. By knowing what you need, you can carry out your plans perfectly, professionally and passionately. Know your target group, know their problems and ask about their needs so that you can meet them exactly. Invest in marketing so that people know about you; build your platform where your potential clients can access answers to their questions and needs. It is important to trade professionally. Do not regret investing money and time to make things professional.

Chapter 4 Herbs For Candle Spellwork

B y the time human beings arrived on Earth, the plant kingdom was well established and thriving. So, it is probably safe to say the herbs are among the oldest tools of magic still in existence today. Shamans, healers, and medicine men and women have long used herbs to restore physical and spiritual health to their patients. And in ancient times, the healing ritual was often accompanied by prayer or an incantation to ask the gods for quick results. This usage was in a time when the world was being illuminated by the Sun, the Moon, and candles. So, it is fair to say that candle magic using herbs has been around since the dawn of time.

Plants get their power from the elements as they grow, and the elements are responsible for creating and sustaining plant life. The little seed grows in the soil of the earth. Water nourishes the seed and prompts its growth. Fire from the sun helps the seed to grow and also turn its carbon dioxide into useful oxygen for the air. And the spirit in the air carries off new little seeds to begin their growth and continue the cycle. Plants and herbs carry natural energy from the universe, so they make a perfect companion to candles when you are performing your candle magic.

The best way to add your energy to your candle magic is to grow your herbs whenever possible. Start with just a few herbs that you might already know and go from there. Herbs are not difficult to grow from seeds or cuttings and can easily be grown indoors in pots, as well as outdoors in a garden plot. And growing your herbs will allow you to charge them with your energy from the time they are seeds or cuttings. If you do not have green thumbs, don't worry; it is perfectly acceptable to purchase your herbs from someone who knows how to grow them properly.

Herbs are very well-suited for use in candle magic because they carry powerful properties that will magnify and enhance the power and effect of your magic spell. There is an herb available to use with almost any type of spell that you might be casting. You can use herbs in various ways during your spellwork. You can rub the candle with the herb or allow the herb to charge the candle. You can make a sachet of an herb or an herb blend and use it to scent your altar while you work your spell. Herbs can be used in diffusers to lend a certain aroma to the room that the altar is in. Drop a few sprinkles of the herb in a burning incense or a candle flame. By using herbs, you will harness the energy and power of the herbs and use them to enhance and magnify the power behind your spells. While it is not required to use herbs for candle magic, it will make your spells so much more powerful and give you better results.

Know your herbs before you use them. Some older spells still use herbs that are toxic or poisonous. If you work these spells, be sure to handle the herbs with great care. If using these herbs makes you uncomfortable or fearful, then do not do that spell, or you can substitute a comparable herb for the toxic one. There are always other herbs that can be used for your candle spells.

Here are some common intentions that you might be casting a spell for and the herbs that will work well with that intention.

INTENT	CORRESPONDING HERB
Abundance	Walnut, blackberry, Vervain, chestnut, rice, corn, poppy
Accidents	Wormwood, feverfew, aloe
Addiction	Plantago, almond
Agriculture	Poppy
Anger	Alyssum
Animals	Valerian, nicotiana, larkspur
Aphrodisiac	Water lily, agapanthus, saffron, blackberry, garlic, cloves, damiana
Astral Projection	Mugwort, magic mushroom, motherwort
Aura	Yarrow, pennyroyal
Babies	Yarrow, angelica, fir
Balance	Sunflower, alyssum, okra, enchanter's nightshade
Battle	Masterwort
Beauty	Holly, aloe, heather, apple, evening primrose
Beginnings	Saffron, birch, narcissus, crocus, heather
Binding	Unicorn plant, bindweed, indigo, enchanter's nightshade

Blessing	Rosemary, angelica, rice, anise, juniper, cinnamon, hyssop, hawthorne
Blood	Pokeweed, bloodroot
Business	Basil
Calm	Alyssum
Change	Solomon's Seal, maple
Childbirth	Geranium, fir
Children	Blue Cohosh, birch ,
Clairvoyance	Angelica
Clarity	Fir, eyebright, cardamom
Cleansing	Yarrow, bloodroot, sage, cloves, rue, comfrey, rosemary, lemon, pennyroyal, marsh mallow
Communication	Yew, mint, yarrow, parsley
Conception	Mistletoe, bistort, geranium, chestnut
Confidence	Sunflower, fennel, motherwort
Courage	Yarrow, black cohosh, thyme, fennel, phlox, masterwort
Creativity	Walnut, mandrake, tomato
Dreams	Yarrow, ash, wormwood, bay laurel, thyme, damiana, poppy, hazel, oregano, holly, mugwort, honeysuckle, mint
Eloquence	Joe Pye Weed, cardamom, fennel, chestnut

Employment	Evening primrose
Energy	Lemon, allspice, ginger, ash, astragalus, chestnut
Friendship	Evening primrose, cloves, crocus
Fidelity	Rosemary, apple, comfrey, basil, bay laurel
Fertility	Olive, oak, almond, narcissus, apple, mistletoe, monarda, arnica, mayapple, asparagus, mandrake, birch, chestnut
Gratitude	Bluebell
Generosity	Honeysuckle
Happiness	Rose, basil, pelargonium, geranium, oregano, mandrake
Harmony	Phlox, basil, marjoram, bloodroot
Healing	Violet, rose, allspice, aloe, pennyroyal, oak, bay laurel, cinnamon, maple, echinacea, cloves, comfrey
Health	Pine, angelica, pelargonium, hawthorn, oregano, oak
Home	Wolfsbane, African violet, thyme, olive, aloe, basil, betony, chrysanthemum, chamomile
Honesty	Bluebell
Inspiration	Hazel
Insight	Walnut

Intuition	Honeysuckle, chestnut, goldenrod
Joy	Sunflower, eyebright, pine, marjoram, oregano
Knowledge	Hazel
Leadership	Sunflower
Longevity	Chestnut
Loyalty	Sweet pea
Love	Geranium, almond, aloe, forget me not, evening primrose, crocus, bluebell, cinnamon
Luck	Poppy, allspice, almond, oregano, oak, ash, cloves, honeysuckle, goldenrod
Marriage	Rosemary, apple, rose, birch, marjoram, bloodroot, hazel, hawthorn
Meditation	Enchanter's nightshade, acacia, damiana, anise, chamomile
Money	Rice, poppy, alfalfa, allspice, oak, nutmeg, almond, basil, mandrake, goldenrod, chamomile
New Beginnings	Saffron, birch, narcissus, crocus, heather
Optimism	Water lily, pine
Passion	Tomato, garlic, parsley, ginger
Peace	Violet, alyssum, olive, basil, narcissus, chamomile, crocus

Power	Acacia
Prosperity	Pelargonium, alfalfa, bayberry, mayapple, mandrake, blackberry, hazel, goldenrod, cloves, echinacea
Protection	Bloodroot, burdock, acacia, agrimony, basil, bay laurel birch, amaranth
Psychic Abilities	Saffron, acacia, rue, monarda, agrimony, mandrake, bay laurel, honeysuckle, bistort, garlic, dandelion
Purification	Sage, birch, rosemary, chamomile, okra, devil's claw, lemon, juniper, lavendar
Relaxation	Lavender, damiana
Release	Comfrey, chamomile
Renewal	Thyme, birch, narcissus
Romance	Tomato
Sleep	Thyme, agrimony, poppy, anise, eyebright, betony
Spirituality	African violet
Stability	Oak
Strength	Thyme, chestnut, saffron, plantago, garlic, masterwort, pine, mint, parsley, oak
Stress	Marjoram, damiana, lavender
Travel	Yew, basil, pennyroyal, comfrey, nutmeg, feverfew, maple, heather, lungwort

Truth	Bluebell
Visions	Wormwood, angelica, marigold
Wealth	Walnut, blackberry, vervain, eggplant, saffron, heliotrope, honeysuckle
Wisdom	Solomon's Seal, apple, sage, hazel
Youth	Tansy, anise

While there are probably hundreds of different herbs available for use by those doing candle magic, you will probably find that you are naturally drawn to the same few over and over. These are the herbs that have proven that they are useful and effective for working candle magic.

- SAGE – Sage is available loose-leaf or dried and crushed. It is the most popular herb known for cleansing your personal space and removing unwanted negative energy. Sage can be used in rituals to welcome new possessions that you want to cleanse. You will use sage in rituals where you are seeking good luck or wisdom. Sage will also help to heal grief and bring emotional strength when needed. It is also used when you are working spells for protection. Sage grows well in home gardens, even inside in pots, but legend has it that it is unlucky for you to plant your own sage. Either find a seedling that is already growing or have a friend or loved one drop the seeds in the soil for you. And you will need to consider planting something else in the pot with it, such as a few marigold seeds, because sage does not like to be alone.

- ROSEBUDS – Red rosebuds are a must for any spell that is being worked to draw romantic love to you. You can sprinkle them around the altar while you are casting your spell. Every different color of rose has a different magical meaning that the rosebuds will also have. Red is the color of respect and love. Deep pink rosebuds are used for spells for appreciation and gratitude. You will use light pink rosebuds when casting spells that have to do with sympathy and admiration. Desire and enthusiasm spells will benefit from rosebuds from orange roses. You will promote friendship, happiness, and joy with the rosebuds from a yellow rose. White rosebuds are used for spells of innocence, humility, and reverence. When you have rosebuds from a yellow and red blended rose, or you mix rosebuds from those roses, then you will work spells of joviality and gaiety. And any of the pale shades of roses will give you rosebuds for spells of friendship and sociability. Pick the buds early before they open, and do not pick more than you need because then you will have no roses.

- LAVENDER – Witches throw lavender onto the fires during the Midsummer celebrations to give honor to the gods. You can use lavender to make a strong tea to drink after spellcasting. Lavender in a sachet will help to bring the scent to your altar. You can also burn lavender incense or dried leaves of lavender in a cauldron on the altar while you are casting your spell. You will use dried crushed lavender when you work spells to promote longevity, good sleep, purification, clarity of thought, protection, and peace. Lavender is associated with removing harmful entities from your presence and leaving only good things behind. If you want to improve your clairvoyance and your psychic abilities, then work a spell using lavender and amethyst crystal. Lavender is easily grown at home and makes a wonderful edge plant for any garden.

- FRANKINCENSE – This is one of the most ancient of all of the herbs we have available today. Frankincense is a purifying herb, which is why it is often used during ceremonies at church in various religions. You will use frankincense in any spell that you are casting for health, success, joy, courage, strength, purification, and protection. Frankincense can also be used to cleanse your altar space and to help cleanse your tools and candles before spellcasting. It will also help to enhance your psychic abilities. Frankincense will be used in spells that are performed to honor the Sun God or any of the Fire deities. It will attract spiritual vibrations and cleanse you of impure thoughts.

- BAY LEAVES – Bay leaves are also known as bay laurel leaves. Crushed bay leaves can be sprinkled on a burning incense or burned in a cauldron on the altar to bring a marvelous aroma to your workspace. You will use bay leaves when you are casting spells with intentions for prosperity, success, healing, stress relief, or banishing unwanted negative energy. Mix bay leaf with sage to quickly cleanse your sacred altar space. Burn bay leaves while performing candle spells to cleanse your home of the other person's aura after the end of any kind of relationship. Bay leaves grow well indoors or outdoors.

- PEPPERMINT – This is an all-around amazing herb to have in your home. You can brew it into a tea for drinking after spellcasting. Lay peppermint leaves on your altar and enjoys the lovely aroma. You will use peppermint in spells for rest, renewal, healing, passion, prosperity, consecration, good luck, happiness, success, and psychic development. Peppermint is a favorite plant for witches to grow at home because of the many different uses of the peppermint plant.

- DRAGON'S BLOOD – Dragon's blood is a resin that is harvested from the stems and the fruit of the Draconis palm plant. Because the fruits are dark red in color, the resin is also dark red in color, hence the name dragon's blood. You will use dragon's blood when you work spells for cleansing your home, removing negative energies from departed guests or occupants, drive away negativity and evil, protect and purify your home, and build up a protective barrier around you and your home. You can also use it in spells to attract money and wealth, increase courage, attract love, and add to other herbs to boost their own natural power. Dragon's blood is also useful for banishing and healing spells.

- PATCHOULI – Patchouli is probably one of the most misunderstood herbs because of its long association with the hippie culture, whose followers used it because of its earthy smell and its reminders of nature and the land. Patchouli has been in use for centuries as a trade item and to repel insects. It will blend well with other scents like sandalwood, cedarwood, cinnamon, rose, lavender, clove, and myrrh. Use a few drops of patchouli oil on a charcoal burner or light a patchouli incense to give a wonderful aroma to your workspace. You will use it in spells for purification, protection, and banishing. It is also recommended for candle spells dealing with money, success, and love.

SANDALWOOD – Sandalwood has been in use since the ancient trading ships sailed from China to all parts of the world. It is one of the first wood incenses known to man. If sandalwood is not purchased as an essential oil then; it is a wood chip and must be burned with charcoal to release its amazing scent. You will use sandalwood for spells seeking spirituality, purification, healing, and protection. Sandalwood paired with lavender will call down good spirits. If you want peaceful dreams, you will pair sandalwood with jasmine. And sandalwood with frankincense is used to consecrate tools and candles.

Once you have decided which herbs you would like to keep at home, and you have begun to build your collection, you must pay careful attention to the storage of those herbs. It is best to keep your herbs in a place that is dry and cool. This will keep them fresh longer, and sunlight will wither herbs and kill their potency and power. Too much moisture and heat will make your herbs moldy. You can keep your herbs in the plastic bags they arrived in, or you can transfer them to glass jars. Whichever method you choose, just make sure it works for you and that your herbs are easy to get to when you need them.

Chapter 5 Seasonal Spells

There are laws of nature that are fairly constant. The sun will always rise and set. Days must always pass to weeks and weeks to months and then to years, decades, etc. There is always a time for winter and autumn. Life and time are constantly progressing and, irrespective of what anyone thinks of them, they will still pass anyway. This cycle is the music to which the ancients dance. Carefully mastering seasons and following through from we have learned from them increases the quality of our lives and also helps us keep up with the constant demands of life.

Timing Magic

It is not news that the rise of modernism has made a dint in the way we do things. When we have a look at the different types of calendars, you'll see the lunar cycles or the precise time and also information about when another season starts. This is good. But this information alone does not have the power to eradicate the value of study of modern magic and perception. We can take a glimpse at what our ancestors taught us prior to their passage into the land beyond and the various techniques that we can use to apply them in determining the timing of certain functions such as spells.

The Magic of the Moon

The night sky is the only source of reliable light and guides and seers are always on the lookout for the moon for some kind of symbols on which they designed their everyday rituals and life. Every shape that the moon assumes has its own meaning, from the quarters that it forms to its fullness. For each month, the

186

moon of that month has a given name that is appropriate to the tribe, culture, or climate. This name goes a long way to explain something about the cycle of the earth or the activities of the people at the time of the appearance of that moon. When thinking about cooperative magic, the name is only a starting point.

Names of the Monthly Full Moon

January: Chaste Moon, Wolf Moon, Quiet Moon, Snow Moon, Manitou Moon, Frost Moon.

Application: The full moon of January may be the appropriate time to think about the power of silence. This is for your mental health and not just for the sake of meditation. We can better listen to the Divine voice and the voice of our Higher Self when we are quiet.

February: Soft Earth Moon, Trapper's Moon, Cleansing Moon, Starving Moon, and Light Returns Moon.

Application: February's Cleansing Moon provides you with the privilege to purify your magic tools ritually (you can also get to purify your own aura). It is interesting to note that the Romans dedicated the whole month of February to these types of cleansing.

March: Flower Time Moon, Fish Moon, Worm Moon, Storm Moon, Plow Moon, Seed, and Sap Moon.

Application: Those who live in the Northern Hemisphere can make use of the energy of the Plow and Seed Moon for making their own magical concoction. Look for modest indoor containers for the plants you choose and bury those seeds in the soil on any day that is sunny.

April: Leaf Spread Moon, Egg Moon, Planting Moon, Pink Moon, Budding Tree Moon, Water Moon.

Application: Take your seedling from the Plow and Seed Moon and place them outdoors when the weather is warm. Or you can also arrange a feast for the Egg Moon that offers sunny-side-up eggs (bringing in the warm solar energy).

May: Hare Moon, Milk Moon, Corn Planting Moon, Ice Melting Moon, Joy Moon, Dryad Moon.

Application: You should think about using some dairy products in an edible spell or a potion in May during the Milk Moon. Milk has the potential to nurture energy.

June: Honey Moon, Strawberry Moon, Rose Moon, Hoeing Corn Moon, Fat Moon, Lover's Moon.

Application: During the full moon of June, it is always certain that the atmosphere is full of love. You should get busy working your spells and rituals that support your relationships.

July: Blessing Moon, Raspberry Bualo Moon, Breeding Moon, Go Home Kachina Moon Thunder Moon.

Application: During July, the Raspberry Moon symbolizes kindness. What signs of good do you intend showing your mates, friends or neighbors?

August: Woodcutter's Moon, Grain Moon, Mating Moon, Gathering Moon, Harvest Moon, Dispute Moon.

Applications: August starts with the ingathering. Now is when you will have to be reaping blessings from your efforts if you have been working on a personal or spiritual goal.

September: Barley Moon, Hunter's Moon, Little Wind Moon, Spiderweb Moon, Wood Moon, Wine Moon.

Application: Look to the Spiderweb Moon as supporting our communication and networking efforts. September is also the right month to ask yourself, "**What am I tied to and is it healthy for me**?"

October: Changing Moon, Leaf Falling Moon, Blood Moon, Sandstorm Moon, Basket Moon.

Application: This full moon comes with the power to cause transformation. What are the parts of your life that you desire to be changed? Formulate spells for these changes you desire.

November: New Snow Moon, Frosty Moon, Moon, Dead Deer Shedding Horns Moon, Ancestor's Moon.

Application: Does it ever cross your mind to build a familial altar for your ancestors in your home? If this is your thought exactly then set the altar up on November's full moon.

December: Oak Moon, Baby Bear Moon, Cold Moth Moon, Winter Houses Moon, Long Moon, Wolf Night Moon.

Application: Take a look at the sacred place you have in your home. How do you think you can keep it cool and great for magic? In urban settings, your modern designations of moons, their significance and their names may like change all the time. Consider your annual series. What do you think each month symbolizes in the grand scheme of things? Do you intend to spend up to one year studying the events of the full moon on a monthly basis? Look for a short phrase that will explain the activities and the energies that you seem to want the most and apply the idea on the object of your deliberation.

To put this in perspective, say your year starts in January with Staying in Moon; then the following names follow like this:

February: represents Birthday Moon

March: represents Melting Moon

April: represents Mud Moon (or Rain Moon)

May: represents Bare Feet Moon

June: represents Lawn Cutting Moon

July: represents Barbecue Moon

August: represents Harvest Garden Moon

September: represents Children to School Moon

October: represents Prepare House for Winter Moon

November: represents First Snow Moon

December: represents Holiday Moon

You will no longer find it difficult when you make use of the information in annual ritual format.

Stay indoors in January and concentrate on the rituals by looking for integration and also looking within you. The Birthday Moon for February sometimes includes a ritual in the form of birthday blessing. March comes with the snows starting to melt in the north, so where you find an ice cube hold a ritual. Make sure you melt away the ice so that the obstacles in your life can be melted. April, which comes with rain, serves to purify the space for your spells and you should dance in the rain, so perfect your rite.

Shed your shoes and ensure that you revel in solar magic in the month of May. The next month, the month of June, is ideal for you when you want to bond with the earth. Festivals are better carried out in July. The month of August symbolizes an ingathering of first fruits. You should carry out rituals for the well-being of your children in the month of September. When you need to carry out a ritual for protection, then October is the month that you've been waiting for. November is the month when you should give yourself some break from the troubles of daily life and get to reconnect with nature and the world around you. December, which is the last month, should be the time when you reconnect with family members and friends. It is true that your lunar year won't be the same as that of any random person. Change the symbolic values of each month and the name of the month as you become accustomed to the change in your personal activities and your environment at large. When done in this way, your lunar calendar will be a direct reflection of who you are at your core, your place in your tribe and your spiritual being.

It is a known fact that almost all metaphysical traditions have their own seasonal observance. You have absolutely no reason not to follow your own tradition because that means a lot to you. Take a mental tour and consider the meaning it has to you. Carefully think about what each season denotes energetically and physically. What follows here is somewhat generic but then it is also a nice starting point because it contains some spells and charms that show that energy being in an annual cycle.

Spring Themes, Spells & Charms

Springtime is one of the best times for you to renew both your body and soul plus your energy too. Thoughts of romance, happy friendships and playful relationships come with this upbeat energy. This also corresponds to the time of new beginnings, the winds, and the Air element. It should be your major focus to clear the old energies and allow the new energies to fill in. Cultivate and create; be real and truthful. Make use of aromatics, bells, and feathers, in your spells and rituals so as to honor the wind.

The Tickle-My-Heart Spring Talisman

Make a cut of the heart that is small enough so that you can easily carry it. Get ready a feather plus a mixture of marjoram tea and rose water. Take the heart in one of your hands (make sure that you do not overlook the allegory in this action) and make a mental picture of it being tied with pink-white-colored light that appears to prance with delight. Carry the feather in your second hand and carefully dip it inside the mixture. Place it on the heart saying:

"Powers of the spring, sing, oh my soul!

Let it dance with joy; renew romance!

Tickle my heart; playfulness imparts!"

Move this token as close to your heart as possible till you feel led to overflowing with happiness. Try re-energizing it when you no longer feel the need for this token. Give it to someone struggling with the blues.

Festive Flower Spring Spell

Get outside your house in the morn; carry morning glories that are freshly picked and a handful of lavender flowers. Scatter all of them to the wind while moving in a clockwise direction. When the sun shines over the horizon, say:

"Happiness without, hope within

I give this joy to the winds.

As these petals free,

Bring happiness back to me."

Summer

Summertime is really characterized by a rush of activities. During this time, you'll tend to go to the gym, take a vacation, or even visit people you've not seen for a while. Hence this time helps us to build more effective relationships and healthy self-esteem. Be attentive and present. Make use of some resources, candles, and incense to honor the sun in your ritual.

Summer Energy Amulet

In order to start this, you'll need a small gold-plated object. Maybe a golden-yellow-colored AAA battery would make a nice selection due to the fact that it represents the "grabbing" of energy. Go outside on a bright day. Do this before the day turns noon. When it starts to chime, hold the battery up to the light and proclaim the following:

"With the toll of one, this spell has begun.

Come the chime of two, the magic's true.

Come the ring of three, energy to me.

Come the toll of four, the power to store.

Come the chime of five, the magic's alive.

Come the ring of six, the energy−ax."

When the clock sounds six more times, create a mental picture of your token being absorbed by the golden rays from the sun in your mind's eye. Take this along with you whenever you feel your core diminishing from all that social activity. Gently touch it and say, "**The magic's alive,**" making sure that you release some small amount of energy as you make this statement. You should get to recharge your token in the sunlight once you've used it six or more times.

Summer Fires of Rejuvenation Spell

 Take a step outside your house on a bright noon day when the day is still sunny. Take a barbecue grill with you, red carnation petals plus the quantity of bay leaves that just fills your hands. Create a mental image of the sun in your mind and internalize it so much that you begin to feel as though you will burst with energy. Afterwards, release the carnation and the bay while saying these words:

"**As carnations and bay begin to ignite**

So my magic takes to light.

The flames release energy

So the power grows in me!"

Fall

The time is indeed come for the harvest. Autumn is the time of preparation, coolness, and water. Go all out and honor the earth with your innate abilities. Direct your gaze and let it fall on inner beauty; inspire wisdom when necessary. In order to receive, you'll have to give thankfully. This is a basic law of the universe. It is not a man-made law. It predates every law that ever existed and it is obvious that it is not going away anytime soon. You can make use of tears, dew, or seashells to honor the Water element.

Fall Manifestation Fetish

Think of a personal characteristic or an interesting project that catches your fancy and that you'd like to see manifest sometime soon. What you'll need is a representative of the project, a portable container, and a small amount of soil that is rich. Position a hand on the soil and say:

"Ops, goddess of the success and harvest,

See my efforts to_____ [define your aim],

Assist me to secure what I have diligently tended and sown.

Invigorate this fetish by your presence

So that I _____too may harvest like the earth.

So shall it be."

Fall Abundance Spell

You require a flowing stream of water in order to start this. A hose is ok, but a natural source is better. You will also need a collection of dry chamomiles. Find your way to the water source in the noon. Stand and position yourself so that the water flows towards you. Sprinkle the chamomile as far as you can on the upstream water while making this proclamation:

"Abundance flows to me, abundance free flows to me.

Here and now I claim prosperity and success."

If you would like to, collect a small amount of the chamomile from the water and let it dry for a portable charm.

Winter

The winter time is often known as that time when all our thoughts drift towards food that warms our bodies. This period is also characterized by frugality and alignment with the element of Earth. This period keeps us grounded and appeals to our cherished desires; it encourages self-confidence and nurtures patience. Renew and share via the simple act of silence and thoughtfulness. Make use of potted plants, soil and seed to honor the earth.

Winter Health Amulets

Whether you chill in the air or you don't, nobody really desires to stay in a sickbed during a holiday. Make this bundle of healthy amulets so that you will be free from those pains and aches that are associated with winter. Start with bandages inside a box. Allow them to be in the sun for about three hours (the number three is the number for the spirit-mind-body). When the three hours have elapsed, concentrate your attention on staying healthy while taking the box in hand. Say:

"**Not for wealth, nor for love**

All I wish for today is health.

Healthy mind, healthy body.

I bind all sickness by these words!

When 'ere these tokens are kept with me

Bring vitality; banish all illness!"

Store the packages in a safe location and put one of the bandages inside your wallet. Make use of the bandages when you have a feeling of being run down. This typifies that you have applied the magic.

Winter Sustaining Spell

This spell mixes the energy derived from conversation with soil to help increase prudence on the part of the person casting the spell. Start with a wrapping paper that is brown in color, a path earth, or with a coin. Carefully use the paper to wrap the coin. This means that you have preserved it. Then say:

"**A coin conserved, a coin wrapped**

Assist me in keeping resources preserved!"

Plant the paper and coin inside a hole that you dug near your home so that the energy of frugality comes to you. When the spring finally arrives, dig the coin out and carry it with you like an amulet that conserves nances.

Chapter 6 Enhancing Herbal Spells

Obviously, herbs hold a great deal of power on their own. However, there are a variety of different tools that you can add to your spells to enhance the power. In this chapter, we are going to look at how candles, crystals, stones, gems, and meditation can truly add a great deal of power to any spell that you are trying to cast.

We're going to start by looking at the power of candles. Candles are used in just about every magic ritual and spell that is performed. They come in all different colors, and each color will provide you with enhanced power in a different area. You can see the use of candles in just about every culture and religion that is around today.

Candles

When you start to look at the histories of candles in regard to magic, you will find that they are sacred. With their fire, they helped lead us out of the darkness. Candles are also associated with the dead. There are spells that revolve around candles that allow you to communicate with those that are in their afterlife, find treasure, and improve your dream states.

The exact time that candles started being used in magical practices is unknown. You can find documentation of their uses back to the times of the ancient Egyptians. In addition, they have been used throughout basically every culture and religion from the beginning of mankind.

Candle flames were looked at as a thing of mystery. People found that if they stared into the flame and entered a meditative state, they could reach different levels of consciousness. Some were able to connect with the higher powers, and others claimed to be able to look into the future.

Magical rituals involving candles are extremely common. They are used to help manifest spells for love, prophetic dreams, insight, enlightenment, removing hexes, and many other purposes. Candles truly are a major part of the magic.

Pagans have and always will use candles during their rituals. They are frequently put on altars or at the quarters of a cast circle. Frequently we see them being used at the points of the pentagram.

The color of a candle will influence a spell in different ways. Colors have their own vibrations and attributes that need to be taken into consideration if you plan on energizing an herbal spell with their influence. Most people will anoint their candles before casting a spell. Different oils are used to do this. Depending on the type of spell that you are going to cast will depend on the type of oil that you use. To anoint your candle, you simply need to rub oil into it and concentrate on the intent of your spell.

Let's take a moment and look at the different colors of candles that are available. Additionally, we will discuss the type of spells that each color is going to be best suited for. Magical work is enhanced by colored candles because of their vibration.

White candles are frequently used when somebody is casting a spell for strength. They are also fantastic for spells when you are trying to find spiritual truths. Purification or purity spells are also going to be enhanced when you burn a white candle. Many people find that they can reach deeper levels of meditation when they burn white candles during the process.

Additionally, you can break curses and attract positive forces into your life with candle work using white candles.

Pink candles should be used when you are casting spells that have to do with friendship or love. Pink candles are fantastic when you are trying to reach a state of harmony within your life. They can also be used to bring calmness to your home.

Red candles should be used when you are trying to improve your physical health or your strength. Red is also the color of sexuality and passion. So, if you are looking for a boost in your love life, a red candle can help. Some people will also use red candles in protection spells.

Using orange candles can help provide you with courage. They help when you are casting spells for communication. When searching for better levels of concentration, casting spells using orange candles is advantageous. They are also fantastic when you are trying to solve problems that seemed to have no solutions. Orange candles can also be helpful when you are casting spells for the encouragement of oneself or others.

Yellow candles can help when casting spells of persuasion. They help to provide the spellcaster with higher levels of charm and confidence. If you need to enhance your memory or improve your studying skills, using an orange candle can be of great help.

Green is the color of prosperity and money. So, using green candles during spells for one of these two things will be extremely helpful. Green candles are also good when providing someone with a healing ritual. You can also use them when you are casting spells of fertility. Green is also a great color for spells associated with finding better luck.

Blue candles are quite versatile. They are fantastic to use in spells cast for spiritual or psychic awareness. People also use them when casting spells for protection while they're sleeping and peace in their everyday lives. Prophetic dreams can also come to manifestation when casting spells using blue candles.

Purple candles have a plethora of different magical uses. If you are lacking in ambition using a purple candle in your spells can help you find it. Additionally, they're great for reversing any curses that may have been cast on you or your loved ones. Purple candles are great to enhance the speed at which you heal. It also can be used to help you hold authority among a group of peers. If you are looking for the extra power to enhance any type of spell, a purple candle is never a bad idea.

While gold candles don't offer as many uses, they are quite powerful. They are fantastic when you are casting protection spells. Additionally, if you are searching for enlightenment and connection to the universe or the higher powers, using a gold candle in your spells or meditation practices will enhance the power and ease of reaching your desired outcome.

Like gold candles, silver candles don't offer a lot of versatile use. They can be used in spells to improve a person's intuition. They can also help unlock information from your subconscious mind.

Last but not least, let's talk about black candles. They can be used in spells to help reduce the impact of losing a loved one. They can also be used to remove sadness or discord from somebody's life. Black handles are great when trying to deal with negativity or negative energy that is surrounding your life or your home.

As you can see, candles by themselves play a pretty big role in the art of spellcasting. When you add candles to your herbal magic routines, the power of those spells will be enhanced greatly. This will ensure that you are able to manifest whatever outcome you are searching for. Using the proper colored candle and lighting it for the proper amount of time is important. Having spells of the herbal variety mixed with candle magic will yield great results.

Crystals, Stones, and Gems

From the time of the ancient Sumerians, crystals, stones, and gems have then regarded highly. They were found to enhance the power of spells. Regardless if you were trying to improve your health, game protection, or rid evil spirits from your life's crystals, stones, and gems can help in achieving your desired outcome. This was true way back in the day, and it continues to be true today.

Ancient Greek cultures also found that they could harness the power of crystals, stones, and gems. In fact, a lot of the words we use to name these items come from the Greek. These are only a couple of examples of where crystals, stones, and gems have played a role. Basically, every religion or culture has information in regard to the power of these three items.

There was a period of time that these important tools were pushed out of sight. It was thought that their power was that of superstition. As time moved on, experiments we're done to see if crystals, gems, and stones had any effects at all. It was surprising to find that they affected people on a physical, mental, and emotional level.

This helped to rekindle the use of crystals, stones, and gems in magical practices. Old traditions were combined with these newfound ideas, and the popularity of these items soared. Today there are many books, articles, and other works that provide teachings toward the power of using crystals in your everyday life. Crystal therapy and magic can be used to solve a variety of different problems.

It is important to note that there are some differences between crystals, stones, and gems. It is not always simple to figure out what you are looking at, so knowing these differences is important when you are trying to work on a spell. Gems are made from minerals. They are typically very rare. Gyms are pulled from the earth. From there, they are, typically, cut, and polished. Jewelry and other forms of decoration typically involve gemstones. The nature of them can be precious or semi-precious. Diamonds, emeralds, and sapphires are all examples of precious gems.

Regular stones and gemstones are different things. Standard stones will hold some power, but they're not going to be as attractive looking as gemstones. They do not have as much value monetarily nor do they hold the same kind of power that gemstones will. Regular stones can be found in nature, and their power can be utilized right away.

Crystals are a bit different from gemstones and stones. They're always in the form of a pattern. This is how they naturally occur. They are geometric in shape. The angles of the crystal are all in symmetry. Crystals are three dimensional. And the order of them is easily seen this way. You should keep in mind that crystals cannot be gems, but gems can be crystals.

Of the three categories, gemstones are the most expensive. Crystals are somewhere in between common stones and gemstones when it comes to price. This is why many people prefer to work with crystals as they fit into their budgets more easily. You can find crystals in many decorative pieces including jewelry, ambulance, and vases. When you need an extra boost of energy when casting a spell, crystals are a fantastic go-to option.

There is a massive amount of crystals, stones, and gems that are available to you. It would be impossible for us to go through each and every one. However, we're going to look at some of the most powerful and versatile options that are available to you. They can help power your spells with the extra kick you need to find true manifestation.

The first crystal that we would like to discuss is amethyst. It holds a great deal of power. You will find that this crystal is extremely spiritual. When your life is lacking peace or stability, using an amethysts power in your spells will help rid you of these burdens. It is also a good crystal to use and strong spells. During meditation, it can provide you with higher levels of energy to ensure that your focus stays on point. It also helps to promote calmness, which puts you in the correct mind frame for meditation.

Agate is a stone that is quite common. It is fantastic when you are casting strength spells. It will help you find the strength of your mind, body, and spirit. Many uses it when casting spells for courage. It is also beneficial when you are trying to gain control of your emotions. Heightened emotions can make seeing the truth of a situation difficult so casting a spell with agate for a clear mind will allow you to see what is truly going on an accept those truths.

Purification spells can be heightened by using blue quartz. The type of purification, whether it is mental, emotional, or physical, does not matter. This crystal is very calming and can provide you with the words you need to communicate clearly with others.

Clear calcite also has a ton of different magical attributes. There are several different colors of calcite. Clear calcite will allow you to reach higher levels of consciousness and develop spiritually. Golden calcite can be used for spells of relaxation and to help you reach different realms.

Fire agate is a stone that many people will use in spells that are for courage. It is also extremely powerful when used in spells for protection. If you need to adjust the negative thought patterns you have recently been dealing with meditating with this stone can help reverse them. The connection this stone has with the earth is fantastic, so grounding spells will benefit when fire agate is around. The energy that comes from this stone is very calm and provides people with a sense of security.

If your life seems out of balance, casting spells while using green Jade can be helpful. This common yet powerful stone can bring peace to the tumultuous nature of life. It can also provide you with clarity of the mind, body, and soul. It can also be used in spells to bring love to your life. Many find that it also works well when you are casting spells for courage or enhanced wisdom.

A fewer common stone but also a highly powerful one is labradorite. If you are trying to work on your chakra system, it can help you direct energies more easily. It can allow you to find balance more quickly and this will play a role in every aspect of your life. The connection between your physical and spiritual self will be enhanced. When you are searching for a connection with the universe or higher powers through spellcasting, this stone can help.

Moonstone can help provide us with new beginnings. When performing any type of lunar magic, the use of moonstone is advantageous. If you are searching for higher levels of intuition or you are struggling with the changes that happen in life, casting spells that are aided by the power of moonstone can help correct these issues. Many people find that simply having this stone around helps to lift their spirits. It also holds the power to boost psychic abilities and help you connect with your subtle body. When working on ventures of astral projection and lucid dreaming moonstone can also be quite helpful.

As we discussed with candles, stones can add a lot of power to your herbal rituals and spells. When you combine crystals, stones, or gems to the magical workings, you are participating in their energy enhancement can be quite amazing. This is especially true with herbal magic due to the fact that all of these items come from the earth. Their lines of power are intermingled.

Getting to know and building a collection of crystals, gems, and stones are going to help give you the power you need to manifest a variety of different spells. Whether you are working on finding love, peace, prosperity, money, or other wants or desires using herbal spells mixed with crystals, stones, and gems will help to ensure that they come to fruition.

Meditation

We have discussed meditation several times throughout this book. That is due to the fact that it is such a critical element of spellcasting. Meditation should become one of your daily practice is if it is not already. The power that you can build through meditation is absolutely unreal.

When you meditate, your mind relaxes is and you have the ability to start focusing on the world around you instead of what is right in front of you. As you start to do this, you will notice that the energies surrounding you can be manipulated.

You will also gain better clarity an insight into yourself and those around you when practicing meditation on a frequent basis.

Many people find time to meditate throughout the day. It can be done for a variety of different purposes. Some people meditate to find calmness or peace when their day is going less than great. Others use it to center themselves as they start to feel unbalanced. Obviously, meditation is a huge part of magical practices and should be done at just about every stage of spellcasting.

Your herbs and herbal spells all require some meditation time. This will help you to impress your intent on them. When your tools for magical rituals and spells have an intent pressed into them, it will make manifestation much easier. These herbs will absorb your purpose and then release their power to make it happen.

Some people have a hard time getting into a meditative state. For others, it comes simply and naturally. As with all things, if you struggle with meditation, in the beginning, you'll need just to be patient and continue to practice. There is a large variety of guided meditations that are available to you today. Guided meditation can make getting your head into the proper zone much easier.

Meditation is a practice that has been around for basically ever. It is a practice that will continue to be around for generations to come. This is because true enlightenment and understanding of the world will require a calm and peaceful mind, body, and soul. When we meditate on a regular basis reaching this state of calmness becomes much easier.

Chapter 7 Healing spells

I n a similar fashion to spells of protection, there are a great number of spells which are focused on the healing and the betterment of the human body. As a powerful conduit for witchcraft and magic, the importance of good health in Wicca is often underestimated, so being able to cleanse and heal oneself is vital. However, as with many medical concerns, witchcraft such as that detailed below is not designed to replace the advice of a doctor, merely to complement it. You should always listen to the advice of medical professionals.

A spell for healing

This is a great spell for those who are trying to encourage a healing process in others. As a witch and a Wicca practitioner, you will often find that many people are interested in the kind of spiritual, energized healing that this kind of witchcraft is able to offer. Thanks to the power of magic, you can use spells such as these to help with the healing process.

The first thing that you will need to do is to encourage your patient to relax. Just as you yourself have entered into a meditative state in the previous spells which we have covered, you can now demonstrate your learning by encouraging someone to enter into a similarly relaxed mode. Slow the breathing, and allow yourself into what is known as a "neutral mode," in which you are both relaxed.

As you both begin to relax, you should feel the positive energies and warmth enter into the surrounding space. These might be spirits, goddesses, or whatever the various elements of your own personal brand of Wicca might involve. These are the spirits who will be helping you to heal. Encourage your patient to begin talking, expressing the various parts of their life which are positive. Whether it is relationships, their career, or anything else, encourage them to focus on the best aspects of their life, bringing these energies to the forefront.

Remain in a positive and happy state, eliciting these emotions from the patient. Have them close their eyes, and you do the same. As well as speaking aloud, the positive aspects and energies should begin to fill the room with a warmth and a strong healing aura. Once you are happy that these spirits are present and that they are positive, you should begin to encourage them to help with the healing.

Quietly so that your patient doesn't hear, begin to list the issues which are afflicting the patient and on which you wish the spirits to focus. During this time, the patient should be focusing on the positive aspects of their life and the things which they enjoy doing when they are at their most healthy.

If you have practiced the protective spells from earlier in this book, begin to create the positive shield using an aura of light. Rather than limiting this to protecting yourself, however, imagine that the light is reaching out from beyond you and layering over the patient. This healing energy will be able to not only prevent negative energies from infiltrating your patient, it will also help remove the negative aspects that might be hindering the healing process. Continue in this fashion. After five minutes, you and your patient should both begin to feel empowered and protected. Thanks to the layer of positivity that has descended over you both and the protective shield that has been created, the spirits that you have invoked should be able to help you with the healing process. Once this is complete, begin to encourage you both out of the meditative state. Talk softly and guide your patient back into the room now that they have been cleansed and protected. If needed, you can repeat this process once a day in order to bring the best kind of positive energy to your patient's life. As well as this healing process, the presence of nature in the patient's life is very much encouraged. It is not uncommon to find that many of those whose healing is slower than they might like have very little interaction with nature. This can be as much as adding a houseplant or two to their home or simply walking through a park. Try to suggest that they strengthen their bond with nature in as many ways as possible as this will boost the effectiveness of your own efforts.

A cleansing ritual with the power to heal

Just as a cleansing ritual can be used to protect against negative and untoward spirits, these kinds of rituals can also be used to help remove similar energies from the body and to assist with the healing process. When you are worried about an illness or are not feeling great, then it can often be helpful to ensure that you are correctly cleansed of these kinds of auras. In order to accomplish this, follow these steps. You will need:

- Incense to burn (sage, preferably)
- A single candle (ideally silver or grey-colored)
- A sprinkling of sea salt
- A chalice or cup filled with water (tap water is fine)

Respectively, these items represent the four traditional elements; earth, air, fire, and water. Place the candle in front of you in a quiet room and light the candle and the incense. Begin to settle into a meditative state and remember that the more relaxed you are, the more effective the spell becomes. For those who are feeling ill or under the weather, this can be a difficult step, but being able to temporarily overcome an illness can be rewarding in the long run.

As soon as you are feeling relaxed enough, you can begin.

As the incense begins to smolder and the scent fills the room, cast your hand through the smoke several times. Allow the smoke to pass over your skin and notice the smell as it fills the room. As you are doing so, say the following words:

"With air I cleanse myself."

Next, hold your hand over the burning candle (not close enough to hurt, but close enough to feel the heat on your palm) and say:

"With fire I cleanse myself."

As you say the words, begin to feel the negative energies and the illness burning and smoldering. Next, pick up a pinch of sea salt and rub it between your forefingers and thumb. Then rub the salt over the palm of each hand and say to yourself:

"With earth I cleanse myself."

Finally, dip your hands into the water and wash away the salt and the traces of sage incense. As you clean your hands, repeat these words:

"With water I cleanse myself."

As soon as this is complete, you can extinguish the candles with your still wet fingers and dry your hands. If done correctly, you should begin to feel the illness and the negative spirits departing over the coming days.

A spell for the release of negativity

If you are still encountering negative and harmful energies in your life, this can have an adverse effect on your health. In situations such as these, the most effective solution can sometimes be to simply ask the energies to leave. The power of Wicca is such that not only will it help you identify these energies, but it will also grant you the power to properly dismiss them from your life. If this is the kind of situation in which you find yourself, then read on to discover the best way in which to deal with these issues.

To complete the exercise, you will need only a quiet room and a red candle. Turn off all of the lights and place the candle directly in front of you. As it is lit, begin to enter into a meditation. While you might normally close your eyes, you should instead leave them open and focus directly on the flame as it burns. As you consider the lit candle, focus on the power and the strength of fire as a general force. This is the kind of power that will grant you the ability to drive out the negativity.

Once you have become fixed on the idea of the fire, then you will need to say the following words out loud to the room:

"Any energy that no longer serves me,

please leave now.

Thank you for your presence.

Now I am sending you home."

The way in which you say the words will matter. You will need to fill your voice with conviction, concentrating on the power of the fire before you and turning this power into the tone with which you will drive out the negativity.

Repeat the words, driving them out to the room at large. It can help to visualize the negativity being removed from your body, peeling away like a snake shedding its skin. This is the healing process made real, helping you to find the right energy with which to heal yourself and drive out the unwanted energies.

As you proceed, you should feel yourself becoming lighter and lighter. Once this feeling begins to arrive, you may extinguish the candle and resume your day-to-day activities as you begin to heal.

A healing spell that uses light

We have already mentioned how powerful light is as a force and how it can be used to remove negative and harmful energies from your life. As the final step for those who are searching for a healing solution, light could well be the missing ingredient that you require in order to get the best results. For those who have conducted the previous healing steps, repairing the holes in your aura with light is very important, so read on to discover how it can be done.

Again, find a quiet place to sit and be sure that you will not be disturbed. Using the method of aura creation which we covered earlier, we will repair the holes and will begin with the top of your head. This is perhaps one of the most important areas of the body and will thus need to be healed as soon as possible. Visualize the light resting on your head as a crown, a display of strength which is bound on to the top of your head. Continue to hold this imagine and reach up and touch your head with delicate fingers. In doing this, you will now need to stretch the healing light down over your body. As the powerful aura stretches over your body, it will begin to fill in any gaps and holes which have emerged and which could be causing you issues. Say the following words as you do so:

"I ask that my energy body is filled

with pure healing light."

Use these words several times until you feel confident that the healing process is correctly handled and that your aura has been repaired. Once complete, thank the spirits, the goddess, and the elements, and resume your day-to-day life. If you have been feeling ill, it can be helpful to repeat this process several times in order to better repair yourself while you are feeling at your worst.

An incantation for self-healing

Just as an awareness of the power of Wicca is important, turning this power on yourself can be a great way in which to heal general malaise and worry from about your person. For this particular incantation, you will be making use of ancient wisdom to make the most of the healing properties inherent in the art of Wicca.

More than others, this powerful spell is largely dependent on the abilities of the witch. Even if you do not consider yourself much more than a beginner, practicing and perfecting this spell can be essential if you wish to use Wicca to self-heal. As well as this, it can be best used in combination with modern medicine, exacerbating the effectiveness of the drugs which your doctor is able to provide.

The first thing that we will need to learn is this mantra. This collection of words has been passed down and has become known among many Wicca users to be one of the best ways in which to heal a body. Consider these words:

By Earth and Water,

Air and By Fire,

May you hear this wish,

Sources of Life and Light

Sources of the day and of the Earth,

I invoke you here,

Heal my body and mind.

Learn them by heart, and be sure to use them whenever you are feeling anything other than your best. The words will help to refocus your energies and drive the power of Wicca's energies to help heal the witch's body.

Bringing harmony and peace to an infected space

While it might seem that the body is the element most in need of healing when a person is ill, it can also be useful to heal spaces. By bringing harmony and peace to a room or home, you can accelerate the healing process and ensure that you have the best environment possible to recover.

It can even be used in outside spaces, though the effectiveness might be limited by both the power of the spell caster and the size of the space available. To carry out this incantation, you will require potted plants of the following herbs:

- Rosemary
- Thyme
- Cinnamon

If you cannot get access to these materials, dried herbs and a generic potted plant can be used though they will not be as powerful. The aim is to transfer the power of the spell into the living plants and to allow them to grow and flourish in the space that needs healing.

First, arrange the potted plants in front of you in a line. If you have just one pot, then place that directly in front of you, making sure that the soil is within reach of both hands. Cast your palms over each of the pots in turn (or over the dried herbs) and say the following words:

Balance and harmony,

Peacefulness and ease,

By the Power of Three

All turbulence ceases.

As you are saying the blessing, imagine the energies that you are able to generate as they flow into the plants. The living quality of the soil is becoming imbued with the healing energy that you are providing, which will in turn feed into the roots of the plant. Once complete, you should place the potted plant into the space that you wish to heal.

The spell will continue to work as long as the plant remains healthy and alive and as long as there is one person nearby who is able to occasionally reinforce the positive energies which are present. With these two factors, the plant should continue to provide a lasting healing help.

Distance Healing Spell

Our final healing spell is designed for use over longer distances. As you might imagine, projecting your power over a long distance can be more difficult than close quarter's magic. As well as this, discerning the results can be difficult, so do not be dismayed if you are not able to notice immediate results. Persist with the spell, and refine your abilities.

To complete this spell, you will need:

- Three large candles (white)
- A picture or image of the person who is in need of healing (the more recent, the better)
- A single crystal (preferably quartz)
- A selection of incenses of your choosing.

To begin, place the candles in a semi-circle (half-moon) in front of you. The incense should be lit, placed out of sight, and allowed to burn while you conduct the rest of the spell. Take a hold of the image of the patient and gently place it into the center of the semi-circle so that it is still facing toward you. Place the crystal on top of the picture.

Sit down. Place both of your hands flat against your thighs. Feel your weight moving down through your thighs, legs, and into the ground. Center your weight so that there is a sense of oneness with the ground and the rest of the earth. Feel the healing energies of Wicca driving through you as you breathe, pulled up as you breathe in and pushed down as you breathe out. This is the process of becoming connected to the world and allowing your abilities to travel over a greater distance.

Once you can feel the powers flowing through you, it is time to direct your energy. Take your hands from your legs and hold them above the crystal. Continue to breathe deeply, moving the energies that you have just found into the crystal and driving them towards the intended patient. The crystal is able to focus the energy and direct across great distances. On occasion, you may find that the crystal heats up and increases in temperature. Do not worry if this is the case. It can often be taken as a good sign, though it is not essential.

As you continue to direct the energy, discover the light of the candles as it is laid out before you. Notice the protective ring that they are able to form and focus this energy again through the crystal. The light that is created by these candles is a healing one, one that you are stretching across a great distance.

Finally, imagine the patient as you wish them to be. Imagine them healthy and well, emboldened by the power of Wicca which you have sent a great distance. If you know they are using medicine, then imagine that the drugs are even more effective and that the positive energies that are sent are coating them in a warm glow.

Once this is done. Place your hands back on your thighs and resume a regular breathing pattern. With the incense still burning, extinguish the candles and remove all of the items. The energy which you have sent is complete, but allow the positive emotions to mix with the smell of the incense as it heals the patient.

Chapter 8 Making Candles at Home

The chandler, the village candlemaker, was a vitally important person to villages and kingdoms during medieval times. Since the candle was the only tool for lighting the home at night, the chandler who made the candles were kept quite busy, even though some people made their candles at home.

Today, candles are more of a decorative item than a necessity unless the power has gone out, and there are no flashlights readily available. In the life of a follower of Wicca, however, the candle is still a necessity. It would be impossible to make a candle spell without a candle. If you perform a lot of spells and rituals, the cost of buying candles can be quite prohibitive. But candles are easy to make at home and, after the initial purchase of the needed supplies, fairly inexpensive. Besides saving money when making your candles at home, you will know exactly what is in the candle, and the candle will hold your energy. Making your candles will add a boost of power to all of the spells that you cast.

There are a few basics to making candles at home that you will need to know before beginning. You can make candles right in your kitchen, but you will want something to cover your countertops, such as old newspapers or waxed paper. You can melt the wax on your stove, but you will need a pot to melt the wax in. You can purchase a double boiler for this purpose, or you can set a metal bowl or a smaller pot on top of the pot that holds the water for boiling. You can find inexpensive pots at any thrift store, especially since you will be using them to melt the wax.

There are several types of wax available for making candles, and you can choose to use whichever one works best for you. You might find that you like one type of wax for one kind of candle and another type for another kind of candle.

- Paraffin – People have been using paraffin to make candles for hundreds of years. This product remains the most popular product to make candles at home because it is not expensive, and it will blend with scents and colors well. The only real problem with using paraffin wax is that it is a by-product of petroleum, and some people may find that the scent of the wax triggers allergic symptoms.

- Beeswax – This is the ingredient that has been used the longest for making candles. This product comes from the wax that bees make to live in and produce their honey. This is the reason that beeswax has a natural golden color and a lovely sweet smell. Since bees make it, it is completely natural. This product is not good for adding scents because they might not mix well with the natural scent of the beeswax.

- Soy – Soy wax is made from soybean oil that is blended with paraffin. It is rapidly becoming the favorite for candle-making. Soy wax blends well with colors and scents.

- Gel – Gel wax is a relatively new product that is made from mineral oil and resin. It is easy to work with to make jar candles and votives, but it must be put into a container and will not work for taper or pillar candles. You can add non-flammable items into the gel-like glitter or small seashells, but adding oils for scents is not a good idea because they do not blend well with the gel.

You can buy your wax supplies in pellet or flake form, and this will make the wax easier to melt. Buying wax in blocks is less expensive, but then you will need a sharp knife to cut the wax into small pieces or a grater to shred the wax. Whichever method works best for you is fine.

The success of the candle depends deeply on the wick inside the candle. If the wick is not right for your candle, then it can ruin your candle. The width of the candle is what will determine the thickness of the wick. A tea light candle would use a small wick, while a large container candle will want a thicker wick.

Consider which fragrances that you would like to add to your candles. Of course, you can make candles without fragrance, but then they will smell like burning wax. Again, this is a personal preference; your candle does not need to smell nice to work well. And consider what type of container you would like to make container candles in. Any kind of container that is suitable for a hot liquid will work for a container candle, especially old coffee mugs or glass canning jars, and they make nice gifts. And you will need spoons or spatulas for stirring the wax and a thermometer for testing the heat of the wax. Before you begin melting the wax, cover everything you can with brown paper bags or old newspapers. Wax will get everywhere. You will want to keep a few small Plexiglas cutting boards or glass saucers handy for laying the spatula and the thermometer on.

A taper candle or a chime candle is a dipped candle. Here is a recipe for making two taper-length candles.

Materials needed:

- Candlewick

- A wooden spoon for stirring

- A thermometer

- Some type of double boiler (You can purchase one that is made specifically for wax melting; you can use a small pot on top of a larger pot, or you can set a coffee can into a large pot.)

- One-half pound of plain paraffin wax

- Color (You can purchase liquid, powder, chips, or cakes in most craft stores, or you can use old bits of crayon.)

- Scent oil

Pour cold water into the bottom half of your double boiler. If the wax you are using is not already cut into flakes or pellets, then use a sharp knife to cut it so that it will melt faster and more evenly. Put the wax pieces into the smaller empty part of the double boiler, and set this into the water in the larger pot. Use medium-low to medium heat to melt the wax, stirring it often to help the wax melt more quickly. Keep heating the wax until it begins to boil just slightly. When the wax has reached a temperature of one hundred sixty degrees, it is ready for making the candles. This is when you will add in color and stir well to mix. After adding color, you will add scent, but do not use too much scent. Too much scent will make the candle burn poorly. And when adding the color, don't forget that dry color is slightly lighter than wet color.

Cut one piece of the wick to make two candles. Measure the wick to be the length of the two candles that you wish to make, plus five inches. Leave the wick as one, long piece. Wrap the center of the length of the wick around a wooden spoon or an old pen. Lower the two lengths of wick down into the wax. Dip the wick into the wax deep enough to make the candles the length you want. Lift the wicks out of the wax, and let them straighten out and cool in a minute or two. Dip them into the wax again, and let them cool. Keep dipping and cooling until the candles have reached the thickness you want. Then use a knife to cut the bottom end of the candle so that it is as straight as possible. Hang the candles, and let them dry for twenty-four hours. Then cut the candles apart, and cut the wick to the desired length.

To make a container candle, here are the materials needed:

- Container for the candle
- Old pen or pencil to hold the wick
- Wick with stabilizer
- Double boiler
- Candle color
- Candle scent if desired
- One-half pound of paraffin wax
- Bamboo stick or skewer

Melt the wax using the same method as above. The wick stabilizer is a small round piece of metal that will hold the wick in place at the bottom of the candle. While the wax is slowly melting, glue the wick stabilizer onto the wick. Set the stabilizer in the bottom center of the container, and wrap the other end around the pencil or old pen to hold it steady. When the wax has completely melted and has reached a temperature of one hundred sixty degrees, then add in the color and the fragrance. When the candle is the desired color and scent, carefully pour the melted wax into the container while trying to keep the wax stabilizer in the center of the bottom of the candle. Don't fill the container to the top, but leave an inch unfilled. Let the candle set for a while and then check for sinking. Sometimes, candles will sink in the middle and form a crater. If this happens, reheat the leftover wax and fill in the center. Let your candle sit for at least twenty-four hours, then trim the wick and store the candle or enjoy it.

If you want to make a pillar candle, you will make it the same way that you make a container candle, but you will need some shape of aluminum or silicone mold to pour the candle into. Heat the mold before pouring the hot wax into it because hot wax poured into a cold mold can develop air bubbles on its surface. When the candle has set for twenty-four hours, you can remove it from the mold and trim the wick.

Candles are important tools for any witch but especially for one who likes to work candle magic. And candles are not difficult to make at home with a few proper tools and a little bit of time.

Chapter 9 How Can I Use Crystals to Reduce Stress From Work?

With the use of healing crystals, you can manage everyday stresses effectively while minimizing their effects on your physical, emotional, and spiritual wellbeing. Making use of stress-relieving healing stones in the workplace will ensure that you achieve maximum productivity. It will also help prevent your inner turmoil from affecting your relationship with your co-workers and your clients.

Recommended Crystals for the Workplace

- Amber

Amber stones are effective in providing you with the necessary courage for establishing relationship boundaries. So, if you're the type of person who's not very good in maintaining employer-employee borders or if you're having issues with your relations with clients, then consider owning this gemstone.

- Emerald

This gemstone symbolizes abundance. Use this to achieve mental clarity while visualizing wealth and prosperity.

- Amethyst

When you find it particularly challenging to control a current work situation or when you would like to alter unwanted realities in your workplace, then an amethyst can serve as a valuable ally.

- Purple Fluorite

Place a cluster of these stones right next to the computer to shield you from the negative effects of its electromagnetic field.

- Garnet

If you feel like the energy levels in the office are a bit low, a garnet can help boost that overall energy.

- Blue Lace Agate

If you find it difficult to communicate with co-workers, clients, or persons of authority, the Blue Lace Agate can help you improve your communication skills. Furthermore, it will provide you with courage to speak the truth. Use this stone when you feel like you're voice is often unheard and misunderstood.

- Bloodstone

This gemstone is perfect for individuals seeking more motivation. Running out of brilliant ideas lately? This crystal will help enhance your creativity.

- Smoky Quartz

The workplace can be filled with emotional vampires, from your toxic co-worker to your verbally abusive boss. Use this gemstone to protect yourself from this draining of energy. This gem will assist you in being more emotionally secure and shield you from self-doubt.

- Citrine

The Success Stone is helpful in improving your problem-solving skills.

- Larimar

This is the ideal crystal to be used for opening communication pathways within the workplace. Use this when you're having difficulty listening to and understanding others around you.

- Rainbow Obsidian

Been forgetful lately? This gemstone is recommended if you wish to improve your memory. It will prevent you from missing important meetings and skipping important stuff in your to-do list.

How do I use these crystals?
You can harness the energy and the stress-fighting effects of these crystals in the workplace in many ways. As previously discussed, you may carry the stones in your pocket or fasten them inside your clothes. Alternatively, you may use them as worry stones.

Another way is by placing the stones on your desk or in a sacred place in your workstation where they will be visible to you most of the time. Every time you look at these healing rocks, they will serve as a constant reminder for you to achieve mindfulness in everything that you do.

One more method is by creating a healing crystal grid in your workspace or in your home.

How to Make a Crystal Grid

While healing crystals are powerful on their own, crystal grids are able to combine all the energies of multiple healing stones as well as their scared geometries with the power of your intentions. As such, this yields quicker, more effective results.

The primary step in creating a crystal grid is to identify your intention. Is your goal to invite wealth and abundance? Do you want to maintain your health goals and to reduce stress? Do you want to be able to sleep better at night? The crystals that you will choose to include in your grid will depend greatly on your goal. For instance, crystal grids dedicated for the purpose of health and wellness should make use of mostly blue and purple crystals like Fluorite and Sodalite. Alternatively, you may trust your instincts and select stones that speak to you. You'll notice that when you purchase crystals from a store, certain crystals' energies communicate more strongly to you than others.

- In order to create your healing crystal grid, you need to select a location in your home or in your workspace. Make sure that it is somewhere where the grid won't be disturbed.

- Then write down your intention on a piece of paper. The more specific it is, the better.

- Clear the energy of the room by burning some sage or by placing a bowl of sea salt in the room. This is to make the space suitable for your grid.

- Then, place the piece of paper with your intention right in the middle of the crystal grid cloth.

- Afterwards, take a deep breath and speak out your intention. Alternatively, you may choose to envision your goal in your mind's eye.

- There should be a center crystal that is placed right in the middle of the cloth. To arrange the surrounding crystals, start from the outside moving towards the center. With each crystal that you place, make sure that you are thinking of your intention. Then, place the center crystal on top of the piece of paper.

- The next thing to do would be to activate the crystal grid. This is done by using a quartz crystal point. Beginning from the outside, you should trace an invisible line between each of the crystals to link each stone with the one beside it.

- Finally, you may choose to add candles to enhance the effect of your crystal grid. Allow it the grid to stay in place for at least forty days.

How to Cleanse the Healing Crystals

To ensure the absorbing and energy-giving power of your healing crystals, it is necessary to cleanse them on a regular basis. In fact, as soon as you purchase the crystals, it is necessary for you to cleanse them before using them. This is because these crystals have encountered multiple types of energies as they've been exposed to various environments and have been handled by various people.

- One method of cleaning your crystals is by simply placing them under running water until you are able to feel that all the negative energy has been washed away.

- Another method is by allowing the stones to soak in saltwater for several hours or overnight. Afterwards, rinse the crystals in cool running water. However, not all crystals can be cleansed through this process. Gemstones that have water content, metal content, or porous properties like Opal should not come in contact with saltwater. Stones like Lapiz lazuli and Hematite should not come in contact with salt at all.

- You may also choose to cleanse your crystals in salt through the dry method. Bury the stones beneath some sea salt and leave them for a few hours. Don't make the mistake of reusing that salt because during the cleansing, it has absorbed all of the negative energy from the stones.

- For crystals that should not come in contact with salt, you may opt to cleanse them through the non-contact method. This is done by filling a glass basin halfway with salt. Then, get a glass and submerge it in the salt. Place your crystals inside the empty glass. You may choose to add water into the glass just enough to submerge the gemstones.

As time passes, it would not be unnatural for you to observe that your crystals have cracked. This is because that crystal has given up its life for your wellbeing. It has already done its part in absorbing so much stress and negative energy away from you. When this occurs, utter a prayer of gratitude for the crystal.

Chapter 10 Bath Spells

Debt Banishing Bath

This bath is to banish debt, whether you are already in debt and want to shrink it or you are trying to keep from acquiring any debt.

What you need:

4 ounces of baking soda

20 drops bergamot oil

Pinch of white sugar

Tall white candle

Warm bathwater

Instructions

Add the baking soda and bergamot oil to warm bathwater and stir a few times with your dominant hand.

Break off the top of the white candle, discarding the broken piece over your right shoulder, and lighting the remainder. Place it anywhere in the bathroom which will allow you to bathe by candlelight. Once a bit of wax accumulates around the flame, sprinkle the sugar around the top of the candle to burn.

Enter and bathe as you normally would. When finished, discard the top candle piece out your back door.

This bath can be repeated once per lunar cycle as a defense against debt.

Good Business Bath

This bath should be taken if you need assistance with a particular business dealing. A good time to take this would be before an important meeting.

What you need:

3 teaspoons of brown sugar

20 drops blue food coloring

Warm bathwater

Instructions

Add the brown sugar and blue food coloring to a warm bath.

Bathe as normal and visualize your meeting, or any other specific activity related to your business. Picture everything happening as you would like to see it happening.

This bath may be used as often as necessary.

Business Bath for a Specific Need

This bath should be used to help raise money for something specific that you need in your business.

Debt Banishing Bath

This bath is to banish debt, whether you are already in debt and want to shrink it or you are trying to keep from acquiring any debt.

What you need:

4 ounces of baking soda

20 drops bergamot oil

Pinch of white sugar

Tall white candle

Warm bathwater

Instructions

Add the baking soda and bergamot oil to warm bathwater and stir a few times with your dominant hand.

Break off the top of the white candle, discarding the broken piece over your right shoulder, and lighting the remainder. Place it anywhere in the bathroom which will allow you to bathe by candlelight. Once a bit of wax accumulates around the flame, sprinkle the sugar around the top of the candle to burn.

Enter and bathe as you normally would. When finished, discard the top candle piece out your back door.

This bath can be repeated once per lunar cycle as a defense against debt.

Good Business Bath

This bath should be taken if you need assistance with a particular business dealing. A good time to take this would be before an important meeting.

What you need:

½ cup white sugar

20 drops of blue food coloring

Warm bathwater

Instructions

Add the food coloring to warm water and stir counterclockwise with your left hand. Pour the sugar in the water and as you are pouring state your specific need out loud. Such as, "I need to raise money for an office computer." Don't talk an entire paragraph. State your need as simply as possible.

Submerge yourself and spend a few minutes concentrating on this object you are trying to draw. If it is something tangible (and it should be, for this bath) visualize holding it your hands or touching it. Then visualize yourself working as if you have already acquired your need.

This bath can be repeated weekly until your need has been met.

Couple's Bath

This bath is used to promote passion between couples in a romantic relationship.

What you need:

Handful of fresh rosemary

Handful of dried lavender

Handful of dried yarrow

Handful of dried cardamom

Petals of a red rose

Rose scented soap (optional)

Steaming bathwater

Instructions

Add the rosemary, lavender, yarrow, and cardamom to steaming bathwater. Add the rose petals last.

As temperature permits, enter the bath, woman first. Spend your time in the bath looking into each other's eyes, and making sure some part of your body is touching at all times. It is not necessary to talk. This bath works better in silence. The couple should wash each other, with rose scented soap if you have it. Normal soap is fine if allergies are an issue for either person.

When finished, dry off as normal. This bath can be taken by couples at any time.

Third Date Bath

This bath should be taken before a date if you are feeling particularly amorous. Despite the name, the number of dates you have been on is a nonissue.

What you need:

5 oranges

Steaming bathwater

Instructions

Cut 3 of the oranges in half, and squeeze them over steaming bathwater. The other oranges should be placed in the tub whole.

As temperature permits, submerge yourself. Soak for at least 20 minutes. Not only will you smell wonderful, but you will also feel better. Vitamin C (ascorbic acid) is absorbed by the skin, so you will get a physical boost before your hot date.

When finished bathing, rub the oranges across your body and then exit, allowing your body to air dry.

Looking for Love

This bath should be taken when you are looking to find a date.

What you need:

Handful of parsley

5 cinnamon sticks

Petals of 3 red roses

Warm bathwater

Instructions

Add the parsley, cinnamon sticks, and rose petals.

Submerge yourself and bathe as normal. This bath will make you look, feel, and smell more attractive while you go out and meet potential dates.

The parsley, cinnamon sticks, and rose petals should be thrown out your front door once the bathwater has finished draining.

Increase Sexual Energy

This bath can be taken to boost your sexual energy.

What you need:

Ounce powdered Damiana leaf

Petals of a yellow rose

Handful of mint leaves

Quart of water

Warm bathwater

Instructions

Add the Damiana leaf, rose petals, and mint leaves to a quart of water and bring to a boil. Allow approximately half of the mixture to boil off. Once cooled to room temperate, add everything to warm bathwater.

Submerge yourself and spend a few minutes just relaxing in the water. Once relaxed, you may choose an appropriate fantasy to get yourself more in the mood. When ready, bathe as normal.

This bath can be taken as often as necessary.

Strengthen a Romantic Relationship

This bath should be taken to add strength to a relationship that may have some weak spots.

What you need:

Petals of 5 yellow roses

5 cinnamon sticks

5 teaspoons of honey

5 drops of your perfume

Yellow candle

Large bowl of water

Tuesday evening

Your preferred temperature bathwater

Instructions

Add the rose petals, cinnamon sticks, honey, and perfume to the bowl of water and place it in a window that admits rays from the sunrise. If you must place the bowl outside in order to reach the sunrise, cover the bowl with cheesecloth.

At any time on Wednesday after sunrise, add the contents of the bowl to your normal bath. Light the yellow candle and place it anywhere in the bathroom and bathe only by its light.

Submerge yourself and relax. Once relaxed, think of one thing in particular that your romantic partner does for you that you are grateful for. It is up to you whether you later express your gratefulness to your partner.

When finished, air dry, and pinch out the candle.

This bath should be repeated on consecutive Wednesdays for 5 weeks, using the same candle each week. On the 5th Wednesday, allow the candle to finish.

Chapter 11 Forbidden Spells of Black Magic

If someone walking down the street heard you mention Black Magic, you would find that the reaction you would get is incredibly negative—it has this image of being entirely negative and evil, bringing destruction and pain to everyone around. However, this is not true at all: Black Magic, like all great and powerful tools and powers within the world, are primarily neutral—they can be used for good or bad, depending on the intention. Some people may cast Black Magic to create a love spell or spell of protection. This is not necessarily evil, so long as it is not intended to harm other people.

What Is Black Magic?

If you have heard the paranoia that surrounds the evil eye and hexes, which greatly color the opinion of those around you and how they see Black Magic, you would understand why this sort of magic is so frowned upon by those who do not know better. The evil eye and jinxes and hexes are all forms of Black Magic, and they are absolutely intended to hurt other people. However, it does not have to be painful. Evil Black Magic may bring along with it pain, death, distress, or revenge, but it can also involve positive intentions.

Black Magic, essentially, is a negative force. However, that does not necessarily make it evil. For example, is it evil to reflect evil intentions back into the universe to protect yourself? You are using negative magic—you are repelling the energy away from yourself. This is Black Magic, and yet the intention behind it was pure. It was meant to be protective and keep yourself safe.

Black Magic involves the intervention of free will in some way— for example, when you rejected the negative energy, you subverted the other person's free will. You prevented him from harming you, effectively removing that choice from him.

How Does Black Magic Work?

Black Magic toward other people, then, involves forcing your own free will onto someone else, taking theirs away. When you are using Black Magic, you are taking away autonomy, which is something sacred that should never be interfered upon. This magic works through the subversion of another person's intention, creating chaos where it goes, depending on how it is used. Negative forces that act upon the universe, usually through the use of dark energy or the dark arts, can be seen as an example of this, directly separating white or pure magic from the dark magic we are discussing now.

Black Magic Spells:

We will go over a handful of Black Magic spells now, looking at how they work—particularly at three spells that are intended to be used to influence love itself. Considering just how sacred love is to people, this is entirely unproductive. Asserting your own free will over someone else to force their affections is manipulative and will backfire—you cannot force someone else to fall into love with you, and if the previously discussed love spells have failed to provide you with the result you were seeking, it is entirely possible that the person you were hoping to influence actually does not love you and you should leave it alone. However, it is still a good idea to understand these processes. If not to use, you can at least defend yourself from the influence of dark magic simply by knowing that it is out there and should be avoided to begin with. By understanding this process, you can protect yourself from the dark arts once and for all.

Break-up Spell

This first spell is designed to break up other people. It can be done when the individual that you love is in a relationship with someone else, either marriage or otherwise. When you are in a relationship with someone else, you are not likely to be open to an affair, after all. The easiest way than to influence that person is to cause them to break up with the other person. By breaking them up, then you can encourage them to go to you, or you can allow yourself to be the only interest in that person's life. By removing your primary competitor at that point in time, you will be able to ensure that you are actually able to get the end result you hoped for—attracting the other person on your own.

This spell will involve several different ingredients—you will want to accumulate a white and a black candle, sea salt, seven whole cloves, or clove oil if you do not have them, a knife, athame, or pin for carving candles, white clothing for yourself, vinegar, black paper, a photograph of the people you are trying to break up, a lemon, a sterile needle, black string, and seven nails.

This spell will be the most potent if you use it on the full moon, but if you simply cannot wait, any night will work.

Begin this spell by wearing white clothing. Even just a white t-shirt can help you with this process and aid in the destruction of the couple. Begin by casting a circle with the salt. Then, using your athame or pin, carve the Algiz Rune into the white candle. Now, anoint the white candle with the clove oil that you have gathered, or if you do not have the oil, stab the seven cloves into the candle This will be your protection during the ritual, keeping you free from harm as you meddle in dark affairs. Light the candle, casting an intention of keeping you safe.

Now, anoint the black candle, using your vinegar, and then light that one as well.

With the candles lit, take the photograph, and using the knife, athame, or anything else, cut up the photograph, leaving only the faces of the couple and then take the piece of black paper in front of you. Take your lemon and rub it with vinegar before slicing it in half using your athame. Then, sprinkle the fruit with some salt and then use vinegar.

Now, take your sterile needle and prick your fingertip, drawing blood. You will place one drop of blood on both faces, and then take one of the pictures and place it on the lemon's bare fruit. Place a nail through the photo, securing it to the lemon as you do so. Then, repeat this process with the other picture onto the other lemon.

With the lemons in front of you, use the black candle and drip the wax from it onto each. As you do this, imagine the negative energy flooding toward them. Allow your negative feelings to flow toward the couple. Imagine them fighting and their relationship failing. Perhaps they cheat on each other or say things that hurt each other. Then, imagine the positive feelings when they finally do break up. Continue to channel your energy through the candle until you know that you are done. Trust your intuition; it will let you know when to stop. Then, it is time to say the following chant three times:

"Using the power of my mind

And without being kind

I pass this evil wave of energy

To cause you indefinite agony

Bring only pain

Your love will not remain

With the strength of my bloodstained fingertip,

Demolish this relationship

With the strength of my bloodstained fingertip,

Demolish this relationship

With the strength of my bloodstained fingertip,

Demolish this relationship!"

Then, place the candle down and put the lemon halves together while using the nails to affix them to each other before tying the lemon with string. Wrap the lemon in the paper and place it under your bed. Then blow out first the black candle and then the white candle.

The next day, you need to bury the package and the candle somewhere that the sunlight never reaches—perhaps underneath a porch or a thick bush. Then, that night, allow the white candle to burn until it uses the entire candle.

Forced Love Spell

Sometimes, people feel jilted—they feel like they never found unconditional love, which they wholeheartedly believe they may deserve, and they will force the point, asserting their own will over that of the other person. However, this is dangerous, and the other person deserves their own free will, free of your own intervention. Nevertheless, let us look at how to use a forced love spell. In doing this, the other person will be convinced that he or she is entirely in love with you, entirely devoted to you.

This spell will require several ingredients—you will need a red, black, and purple candle, clove incense, and calamus, cinnamon, and myrrh oil. From there, gather 13 rose petals, either black or a very deep red. You will then need several strands of your own hair, and some of your own genital secretions on a cotton ball. For men, this is semen, which can be prepared up to two weeks in advance, and for women involves vaginal mucus on a cotton ball. Then, gather a photo of you, your lover, and a sterile needle. You will also need a red string, a cauldron, and something belonging to your lover.

This spell is best cast on a Full Moon.

This spell will involve you gathering all ingredients, casting a circle, and using clove incense for your own protection.

Then, anoint the candles using first the myrrh oil, then the cinnamon oil, and lastly, the calamus oil. Place them onto the altar and light each one. Now, set the photographs in front of you and begin with the red candle—drop seven drops of red wax onto your picture first, and then on your loved ones. At this point, think about your loved one and how you would feel if he or she was entirely in love with you. Allow your thoughts to create energy and imbue it through the candle and onto her photo. Repeat with the black, and then purple candles.

Then, place your wax-covered candles face to face with each other and use the string to tie them together. This can be rolled or folded, so long as the photos themselves are touching and tied by a string.

Now, place the photos into the cauldron.

Take your petals and drop calamus oil on each petal. Then, drop each petal into the cauldron while saying:

"Your love is strong, your love is mine forever,

It creates a link, a bond too strong to ever sever."

Now, take your sterile needle and prick your finger before dropping blood onto the cotton ball and place it into the cauldron. Then, place the cotton ball covered in genital mucous into the cauldron as well. Now, you need to mix in your own hairs into the cauldron and then the item that you took that reminded you of your loved one.

Place a few more drops of the oils into the cauldron, then drip some of the candle wax from all three candles into it as well. Focus entirely on the unconditional love flowing toward you, gifting you with it. Then, repeat your chant:

"Your love is strong, your love is mine forever,

It creates a link, a bond too strong to ever sever."

At this point, set everything in the cauldron on fire. Make sure that you are somewhere that will not cause problems if you are burning and preferably, do this outside where you will not set off smoke alarms. As you do this, you will release the energy out into the universe. When the items have finished burning, allow them to cool and then bury them, along with the candles, outside next to a tree.

Bring Back an Old Love Spell

This last spell is used to return an old lover. If you have lost an old lover that you desperately wish to have come back into your life, this is the spell to use. Of course, remember, this is a black magic spell, and it is dangerous and does take over your target's free will.

When you do this spell, you want to make sure that the person loved you at some point—you will be able to then encourage the other party to reignite old feelings and miss you. This is so powerful that you may find the other person intentionally seeking you out, rather than making you chase after him or her.

This spell will require you to gather the following: An organic chicken wing, a red candle, a sterile needle, some of your blood, thread, wooden matches, and one sheet of parchment paper.

To begin, start by lighting the candle using a wooden match. Make sure this is with a wooden match specifically and do not use a lighter. Take the chicken wing and use it to trace the name of your lover onto the parchment paper. Of course, you will not really see anything there, but that is okay. What you need is the motion of the writing, allowing you to know that it is there. Then, you must trace your own name right over the name of the lover. Then, using the red candle, drop seven drops of wax across the paper. Imagine you and your lover together once more, laying together and holding each other in an embrace.

Now, take the sterile needle and prick your finger. You will need three drops of blood onto the paper alongside the wax. During the time that you are dropping the wax and blood onto the parchment, make sure that you are focused on your ex-lover. Think about how much you loved your ex and how much you truly wish your ex would return to your side. You want to feel that desire building up as an energy that you can then use to send off into the universe.

Now, build up all of that energy into your lungs, imagining your pining desire filling them, and blow it out, extinguishing the candle and then say:

"Salima Ratiki Bustako"

You will now set the chicken inside the paper, wrap it up, and tie it in a little package, which you now need to bury somewhere outside. Take the candle with you and save it, and then when the next Full Moon arises, light the candle once more and allow it to burn itself out.

Should You Use Black Magic After All?

Black Magic itself is not inherently evil. It is incredibly powerful, which can then lead to it being incredibly dangerous to utilize, but it is not necessarily evil. It can be when used negatively, but that should not be a reason to never use it in the first place.

Everything exists in dynamics between two extremes that represent opposites—this is why we have both creation and destruction. Without destruction, you could not create and vice versa. Without old, there can be no young, and vice versa. Without wet, you cannot have dry. The concept is that one cannot exist without the other, and that is okay. Everything must have an opposite force that exists in order to balance everything out. This means that Black Magic is a necessary part of the world in order to have White Magic. Without this Black Magic, you could not possibly practice your own White Magic.

Think of the yin-yang symbol for a moment—you must have black and white to have perfect harmony, and this is the same with magic as well. This means that Black Magic is just as valid as White Magic, and because of that, there is no inherent reason to avoid it, so long as you are safe and respectful about the free will of other people, it can absolutely be a valid choice to use.

How can Destructive Magic Generate Love Spells?

Now, you may be wondering how magic that is inherently negative and destructive could possibly produce love spells—which is a valid point to raise. However, if everything exists in dichotomies, in which there are destruction and creation, of course, you can destroy love to create love. The human body is constantly destroying in order to create new processes. It is constantly destroying cells in order to create new ones. When you breathe, you inhale and exhale.

Just as there is the natural cycle in which there is birth, life, and death, you can see a similar pattern in love. Just because you have destroyed something does not mean that you cannot create from the ashes, allowing yourself to form something entirely different as a result of the processes.

Think about the phoenix—it dies and then is reborn in its ashes, looking nothing like it once did. This is what you are doing—you may be destroying love, particularly in that break-up spell, but you are also able to create new love, with you. Of course, everything will come to an end and be destroyed eventually—even the Great Sun will eventually reach its demise after it finishes burning itself. This means, then, that the destruction of Black Magic can absolutely generate Love Spells on its own in its own way.

How Black Magic Can Be Helpful

If everything must die to be reborn at some point, then, sometimes, it must be useful to hurry it along at some point. This is absolutely true—think about how you may have hesitations about letting go of a past relationship in which your partner abused you. You are stuck on him, and you know that you should not be, and yet you cannot possibly let go. Should that be allowed to burn out on its own before you are allowed to feel joy and move on in your life? Should you be forced to endure that suffering, that heartbreak, and that unwillingness to move on from your life, all because you are naturally inclined to miss what you loved for so long?

What if that could be sped along to allow you to move into what is truly a loving and deserving relationship? Should you still wait until you are no longer interested in your ex-partner, who hurt you? It would be useful to end that infatuation once and for all to allow you to heal yourself and move forward. In letting that relationship die once and for all, you open yourself up to positivity and the chance for a happier, healthier relationship. That relationship, then, would be your best bet at happiness, and it would be remiss to tell you to suffer in silence until you naturally get over the relationship. No—you should absolutely be allowed to let go.

Letting go of that process would involve Black Magic. Would you do it?

Many people would. Think of other situations in which you may consider destroying something to make space for new discoveries and success. Perhaps you may have a mental block that you need to let go of in order to allow yourself to finally move forward and toward the money and success that you know that you deserve. Maybe there are petty problems that are destroying a relationship that really should not be, and you choose to use Black Magic to eliminate that problem altogether.

Despite the fact that Black Magic is inherently destructive, that does not make it evil. After all, fire is inherently destructive, and it is the single-most commonly used element within this book. The Sun is destructive—it could blow up and destroy us all. However, it would be insane to suggest that the sun ought to be destroyed or banished for being a destructive force. Just because the sun can cause sunburn and occasionally even cancer does not mean that someone should figure out some way to launch a satellite into orbit that will block the sun's light, acting like a constant eclipse.

Keep in mind, if you do decide to use Black Magic, that it can create great and powerful changes in your life. It is powerful and sudden, and when it does suddenly change, it can cause some serious unintended consequences. Nevertheless, the power should absolutely be considered if you feel like you are ready to use them. Just as driving a car could be fatal if you make one wrong move does not discourage you from driving to work every day, you should not feel limited to avoid Black Magic because of the risk. Simply drive responsibly, so to speak, and be prepared. Perhaps even bring someone experienced along to guide you.

Conclusion

Now that we have reached the end of this guide, you should find that the world of powerful magic is tempting and intriguing. With so many different spells to practice and learn, being able to discover the true benefits of the magical world is something that is worked on over a longer period of time.

The spiritual realm has been found to have a connection with the world of modern medicine, differing only in its proceedings. The magic world is as real as the air you breathe. Don't be mistaken, there are worlds in our world and they are experienced only through our belief system. This is what determines your degree of success in spell casting. They provide you with intricate information that is not readily available to everyone else. Magical spells serve as a means of another livelihood apart from what we already have and we can partake of them through innate acceptance. These spells must be accepted as life because they give you an edge in our present world. What you don't believe can't work for you, but it can work against you. It is on this note that you are invited to put your mind to the workings of these mysteries. Looking at the whole universe and its intricacy, we will agree there are higher powers that be and they can be harnessed for our benefit. These spells must be internalized and held in sacredness, following all instructions and directions. There are elements that can be invoked to work for us. We are consciously or unconsciously influenced by the basic four elements (Earth, Fire, Air, and Water) in nature, which provides a medium of communication to the spiritual source. A positive mind will naturally flourish spirit and body in comparison to a negative and bitter mind, which is always in conflict with itself and its environment, characterized by poor productivity. Seek to live in harmony with yourself first; then you can live in harmony with your surroundings. Private victories precede public victories; as such, you must guard yourself from within. In spell casting what you seek to find will be attracted to you and will abide within you. Your state of mind will reflect the quality of your spells. Spells help you stay in tune with nature and awaken the energies within, which integrates with our exterior to provide a desired effect. These magical spells serve as

- A gateway to winning in private before going out into the world.

- A means of control over what goes on in and around us.

- Alternatives to the limitation of conventional medicine.

Spell work is based on principles, which serve as a function of their creation. These principles can be activated by almost anyone irrespective of class, gender, background and literacy. As in music, you need to strike the right chord to get the right note, which only you know to be right or wrong. Ultimate precaution must be taken in these exercises and proceedings to sustain results and be in sync (understanding). This ensures we don't lose ourselves to our being.

As a beginners' guide, this book is an attempt to place into your hands the core elements of witchcraft. As you work your way through the various incantations and spells, you should discover that you are becoming more skillful with the art of Wicca in general. What you know about one spell will often feed into the others, broadening your knowledge at every opportunity.

With this in mind, it can be helpful to look at spells as an ongoing learning process. Difficult to master, there is always another spell to be learned and always a better way in which to refine your efforts. For those interested in learning more, the reading notes at the end of this guide can offer further insight into the history and the depths of Wicca. All that remains to be said is that you should enjoy yourself and discover just how rewarding and fascinating the world can be when you know more about the power of Wicca.

Printed in Great Britain
by Amazon

25803901R00148